# Africana Health
# Psychology

# Africana Health Psychology

## A Cultural Perspective

Marilyn D. Lovett

LEXINGTON BOOKS
*Lanham • Boulder • New York • London*

Published by Lexington Books
An imprint of The Rowman & Littlefield Publishing Group, Inc.
4501 Forbes Boulevard, Suite 200, Lanham, Maryland 20706
www.rowman.com

86-90 Paul Street, London EC2A 4NE

British Library Cataloguing in Publication Information Available

**Library of Congress Cataloging-in-Publication Data**

Names: Lovett, Marilyn, author.
Title: Africana health psychology : a cultural perspective / Marilyn D. Lovett.
Description: Lanham : Lexington Books, [2023] | Includes bibliographical references and index.
Identifiers: LCCN 2023007901 (print) | LCCN 2023007902 (ebook) | ISBN 9781793632432 (cloth) | ISBN 9781793632449 (ebook)
Subjects: LCSH: Clinical health psychology--Cross-cultural studies. | Black people–Psychology.
Classification: LCC R726.7 .L68 2023 (print) | LCC R726.7 (ebook) | DDC 616.001/9–dc23/eng/20230419
LC record available at https://lccn.loc.gov/2023007901
LC ebook record available at https://lccn.loc.gov/2023007902

# Contents

# Acknowledgments

This book is dedicated to the ancestors, including John Claude Lovett III (my brother), Mary L. Duhart Lovett (my mother), Mama Letha, Dr. L. W. Neyland, and Dr. Kobi. A special shout-out to my husband, Jarvis Hampton, who has given me the space to do my best work, and to our children: Nyasha, Bethany, and Josh. May my family of origin continue to honor the mind-body connection, in addition to the rest of my extended family, fictive kin, and friends. My spring 2022 Africana Health Psychology class deserves special recognition, in addition to students in my African American Health Psychology classes at Livingstone College. Many thanks to the reviewers who provided valuable feedback. Much appreciation to my first editor, Kasey Beduhn, for being understanding throughout this process; to Judith Lakamper, my second editor, for her pointed deadlines; and to Jasper Mislak, my current editor, who helped me make my first book a reality. Last, but not least, peace and blessings to Dr. Reiland Rabaka, my dear friend and brother who always believed in me.

# Introduction

The purpose of this book is to focus on variables related to health promoting behaviors, using a culturally grounded perspective. Talking about health and wellness beyond illnesses sets the stage for solution-focused discussions. Doing so is a nod toward a number of positive outcomes such as academic achievement and drug resistance found to be related to racial socialization and associated factors such as cultural identity.

The aim of this work is not to compare Black populations with other populations, but to focus specifically on populations of African descent. The term *populations of African descent* is being used because it encompasses those who consider themselves Black, whether biracial, of Caribbean origin, or Spanish speakers. *Caribbean* does not automatically mean Black. It is diverse, thus the focus on African Caribbean populations whose ancestors endured slavery or colonialism. Throughout this work, I will use the terms *African-descended people*, *people of African descent*, and *Black* interchangeably.

Black culture is what was practiced by one's African ancestors, as outlined by Linda James Myers (1993), and includes spirituality, collectivism, and communalism. Kambon (1998) discussed other aspects such as harmony with nature, interdependence, and collective responsibility. French and colleagues (2006) found no differences between African American and African Caribbean youth who were followed over three years on collective self-esteem and ethnic identity exploration. Blum et al. (2003) assessed the health status of adolescents in the Caribbean, most of whom were residents of Jamaica, Guyana, Barbados, and the Bahamas, of mostly African descent. Their ages ranged from 10 to 18. The researchers suggested that their findings mirrored those of Black youth in the United States. Parent/family connectedness was a protective factor for youth under the age of 16. However, religious beliefs were protective for those 13 to 15 years old and attending religious services was protective for those above the age of 16. This is part of the rationale behind my using these terms interchangeably.

Much of the discussion regarding African-descended people and health psychology focuses on health disparities. However, doing so misses the rich tapestry of the experience of Black populations and tends to endorse a deficit

1

model. By focusing on comparisons and ensuring that African Americans, for example, get equitable treatment with European Americans misses the leaking boat that is emblematic of the American health care system. Another disadvantage of focusing on health disparities and bringing norms in line with what is going on for European Americans is that it makes them the norm for what ought to be (Madhere et al., 2009).

One way of looking at how this misses the forest for the trees involves an examination of maternal death rates. Recent television shows have spotlighted the deaths of African American women in the aftermath of giving birth. While discriminatory behavior of doctors may contribute to the women being ignored when they were in distress, the fact that women in the United States continue to die in childbirth in 2020 is a problem (Galloway, 2020). Bringing African American women equitable health care in a system where this should not occur in the first place would only solve part of the problem.

This book will explore variables that African-descended populations have in common. For instance, Singh (2004) noted that "the centrality of black diasporic culture . . . points to the relevance of historical struggles in shaping and reshaping identities" (p. 30). The Black Power movement of one voice coming from a diasporic Africa (Singh, 2004) is key to this. The movement was meant to focus on cultural identity. Culture and history have been used to (constrict) ethnicity; however, for the purposes of this book, they are being used to expand the conversation about health psychology's relationship to Black populations. In that way, this work is interdisciplinary and draws from other disciplines such as social work, sociology, and public health.

In the first chapter, "Disrupting the Narrative," I will discuss where we are at this point in time. It will include a discourse of the COVID-19 pandemic as well as factors to consider in using language meant to promote health.

The second chapter, "A Brief Cultural History," involves an examination of the history of health psychology as it relates to Black populations. Medical mistrust is a key component of health discussions among African-descended people and is rooted in a tenuous past; this will also be included in this chapter.

When examining changes in health status, it is best not to focus on the individual at the expense of cultural factors. Individual level behavior does not do a complete job of explaining how best to promote health behaviors. Lightfoot and Milburn (2009) suggested as much in their offerings about HIV prevention. They suggested that not only culture needed to be considered but also context. When we discuss cultural factors, we should consider issues of racial socialization. More about this will be discussed in the third chapter, "Theoretical Considerations," an exploration of theories used to explain positive health behaviors of African-descended populations.

"Moving toward Healthy Living," the fourth chapter, explores research related to health promoting behaviors of African-descended people. For example, the role of spirituality and religiosity in promoting health has been well documented. Among Black people, differences between religion and spirituality exist, as noted by Ojelade et al. (2011). They describe a case study in which a single African American father raising his son was concerned about his son's mental health. Although they were not considered "devotees" of Ifá, they did embrace its principles successfully toward their healing. Turner-Musa and Wilson (2006) reported findings from Black college students suggesting that those who endorsed health promoting behaviors were more likely to be religious.

This book's focus on protective factors contributes to the literature on positive psychology as it relates to African-descended youth. Over 25 years ago, Howard (1996) noted that personality (i.e., self-esteem), family (extended-elasticity-kinfolk), and community (coalitions, rites of passage) factors should be considered when describing youth development. A culturally based health psychology would include these factors. Howard (1996) also suggested that we need to ask the community how they define what is resilient; this puts us on the path toward operating from a strengths-based rather than risk perspective. This kind of research will be discussed in the fifth chapter titled "Cherishing the Children."

Beliefs play a large part in whether someone thinks they have control over their health. A study by Hekler and colleagues (2008) reported that, among African Americans (whose average age was nearly 62), the medical belief model and their lifestyle were inversely related to systolic blood pressure. Additionally, lifestyle behavior mediated the relationship between belief in the medical model and systolic blood pressure. Lifestyle behavior included reducing salt/fat intake, exercise, losing weight, and getting regular physical exams. This is the type of study which would be included in the sixth chapter on "Empowering the Elderly."

Finally, the last chapter, "Toward a Brighter Day," will include a discussion of future directions in health psychology as it relates to African-descended populations. A culturally grounded health psychology can be used to shape programming and policy. For example, Gondolf and Williams (2001) developed the idea of culturally focused counseling for Black men who batter. They noted, "Responding to cultural issues can easily become a way to diffuse this (personal) responsibility" (p. 286). However, this is because of how it has been framed. If dating/domestic violence and batterer's intervention were re-framed as a cultural issue grounded in morality/ethics of care, then personal responsibility would be easier to embrace, as a natural outgrowth of culture, rather than racial oppression.

And so we'll begin.

# Chapter 1

# Disrupting the Narrative

I have been teaching African American health psychology for years. It was a course proposed and approved by a previous department chair at a previous institution. While I am versed in many issues related to the field of Black psychology, from my undergraduate experiences until today, I had never merged Black psychology with health psychology until I started teaching that course. It has evolved into Africana health psychology, as many of the participants in the studies I read include Black people from outside of the United States.

Initially, the course description was written with an emphasis on health disparities. However, I realized that if we are operating from a cultural perspective, we would have to shift our language. The emergence of the term *health equity* best fits the perspective that is best advocated. Rather than asking "How can we use health psychology to eliminate health disparities?" perhaps the better question is "How can we use health psychology to promote health equity?" It keeps us from viewing the behavior of people of African descent through the lens of a deficit model and encourages us to look at protective factors in Black populations, which are often culturally based and buffer against negative environmental impacts.

Because I am an optimist by default, it was not too hard to focus on the positive aspects of the research included in this book. Generally, however, I agree with Airhihenbuwa and Liburd (2006) that "there is an absence of a language of positive aspects of health behaviors that reveal cultural strengths" (p. 491). I saw this consistently while teaching Africana Health Psychology. Students too often got stuck on the literature review of research articles which is often negative. Then, they take the results and discussion at face value because the previously mentioned research, in addition to some of their past experiences, already primed them toward viewing Black people negatively. Much of the research with Black people does not consider cultural variables when reporting on their health. That is what makes this book different. The research included is examined through a cultural lens, in addition to reinterpreting findings so that we are looking for the silver lining.

If we reconceptualized health psychology of people of African descent beyond disparities, we could focus on what these populations are doing right and how they are addressing any health challenges, in addition to promoting health behaviors usually found among these groups. Ultimately, we need, among other things, a three-pronged approach to enhancing health: (1) health equity, (2) social capital, and (3) examining the impact of racism. Stephens (2009) suggested as much in her discussion about people in Australia. She said that three approaches to studying the impact of racism on populations of color should include qualitative methodology such as phenomenology, ethnography, and discursive analyses. The second prong that I have suggested is social capital but could be translated as empowerment or cultural knowledge.

Stephens (2009) addressed empowerment as consciousness raising, as proposed by Paulo Freire in his *Pedagogy of the Oppressed*. In the case of my focus on Black people, this would certainly apply. Akinwumi (2006) surveyed young people in Nigeria between the ages of 17 and 35. Most of the groups they were a part of focused on awakening the consciousness of the local communities to exploitation by multi-national oil companies. Their shared objective was "the right to control the resources in their communities for the benefit of all of their people" (Akinwumi, 2006, p. 79). The third prong, according to Stephens (2009), is analogous to seeing health equity as best advocated using a social justice approach.

A more complete picture of the health outcomes of people of African descent needs to consider both the impact of racism and cultural identity among them. Some of us have grown comfortable assessing the effects of racism over the past 30 years with the development of scales such as the schedule of racist events (Landrine & Klonoff, 1996) and the daily life experiences scale (Harrell, 1997). Cultural/racial identity scales such as the African self-consciousness scale (Baldwin & Bell, 1985) and the Multidimensional Inventory of Black Identity (Sellers et al., 1998) have also existed for decades. As an aside, cultural identity as a protective factor is seen in other ethnic groups. On the flipside, the impact of racism is also experienced among people of color. Additionally, scales, measures, and assessments currently being developed for Black people would do well to include cultural variables. One study that did so discussed a measure which was developed to assess the possibility of Black mothers allowing their daughters to get the HPV vaccine; it included items related to spirituality and collectivism (Cunningham-Erves et al., 2016).

## SIDE EFFECTS OF COVID-19

Writing this book during the COVID-19 pandemic has been eye-opening in a lot of ways. The death toll from COVID-19 has had a devastating impact on the Black community. In the United States, life expectancy has decreased by almost three years, from 74.7 to 72 years of age among Black men and a bit over two years among Black women (Wamsley, 2021-NPR). However, we have not seen numbers like this in Africa. Some suggested that it may be due to younger populations in many African countries, compared to the West's preponderance of older people. The median age of many sub-Saharan African countries is 18 (Edward-Ekpu, 2021). Others posited that the body's cells may remember a previous virus and may be on guard to take care of COVID-19 when it is recognized (Mukherjee, 2021). It has also been proposed that since there is less testing, then there are fewer COVID-19 numbers. However, that proposition does not hold water because antibody testing still yielded fewer cases, compared to Western countries.

While spirituality is a protective factor for many of African descent, faith without works is not enough. Unfortunately, John Magufuli, president of Tanzania, died recently (March 17, 2021), having supported praying that coronavirus would disappear, in addition to the promotion of traditional medicines (Feleke, 2021). This has ushered in the first Black woman president of the country, Samia Suluhu Hassan. The belief in spirituality by Black people has to include the possibility that the Creator works through both medical staff and traditional healers.

In some countries, traditional healing was endorsed by their governments as adequate treatment for COVID-19. These included Zimbabwe, Madagascar, and Tanzania. Unfortunately, the research showing its efficacy is lacking (Matiasha, 2021).

Many African Americans have been stressed due to the ongoing COVID-19 pandemic. Although the rates of anxiety and depression were low among a sample of Black people from the first year of the pandemic, both of these variables were predicted by variables such as worry about health and living conditions in a study by Asare et al. (2020). Most of the participants were women and married, and little over half were born outside of the United States. Most had some college, were middle income, and had health insurance.

It is still stunning that in the United States, universal health care does not exist for everyone in a pandemic. Although residents are encouraged to sign up for health care on the private insurance market, this has turned out to be unaffordable for many. Because health care is tied to employment in the United States, the loss of a job meant the loss of health care. Thousands of people have died from not having this access.

## TO VACCINATE OR NOT TO VACCINATE

There has been a lot of controversy around vaccinations, some of which had nothing to do with health indicators. Kelly et al. (2021) reported that Black people in the United States were less likely than other groups to get a COVID-19 vaccine were it to become available. Data were collected in early 2020. Months later, the first person to *get* the vaccine was a Black woman, in addition to the first person to *give* the vaccine. It should be noted that insurance status was key in whether one would get the vaccine; it still seems to play a part today, due to unanticipated side effects.

Contrary to popular opinion, the rollout of the COVID-19 vaccine on the continent of Africa includes the benefit of experience among the countries, the African Centres for Disease Control, among others, including WHO and UNICEF. Because they have experience with other vaccines affecting large swaths of the population, this gives them an advantage that other countries have not seen. An important element, trust, has been noted among the medical community and traditional healers (Edward-Ekpu, 2021).

Past instances of successful vaccinations reported by African countries have prepared them for yet another vaccine. One previous example is that of wild poliovirus, disappeared from Nigeria in 2016; millions of children in Chad have been immunized against it as recently as November 2020. In Ghana, guinea worm disease has been eradicated due to a few organizations such as Dr. Sulley Gariba's Institute for Policy Alternatives and former U.S. president Jimmy Carter's Guinea Worm Eradication Program at the Carter Center (KobigBilla, 2021). Thus, many African countries reported that their respective populations were willing to receive the COVID-19 vaccine. The first COVID-19 vaccines arrived in South Africa in February 2021 (Edward-Ekpu, 2021).

The narrative has been that the rest of the world does not have vaccines when the truth is that they have vaccines that they are making themselves, but these are not recognized by Western countries. To add insult to injury, the United States issued a ban against those traveling from countries in southern Africa due to their reporting the existence of the Omicron variant of COVID-19. Omicron was also found in Israel and South Korea, but those countries were not restricted by travel bans (which were ultimately lifted).

Another part of the story that is missing is the availability of the COVID-19 vaccine beyond Western pharmaceutical corporations. Attempts have been made to generate vaccines in various African countries. However, there are three reasons this has yet to occur. For one, because European-based countries of the World Trade Organization opposed lifting intellectual property protections, developing countries were not able to make the vaccine using the patented technology. I use the term *developing* not to indicate that those countries are not developed but to recognize how imperialism has prevented progress in what were previously known as Third World countries, by design. Edward-Ekpu (2021) reported that funding for vaccine production on the continent was hard to come by. Secondly, many African governments gravitated toward ready-made vaccines, as it is cheaper than vaccine development, including clinical trials. Due to the relationship between many African countries and China, there is a vaccine from China being disseminated in countries such as Zimbabwe (Matiasha, 2021). Third, Dr. Christian Happi, head of the African Center of Excellence for Genomics of Infectious Diseases in Nigeria, believes that the attitude and behaviors of these governments can be attributed to colonizing effects. He stated, "We have the human resources, we have the know-how; we have the intellectual capacity, but we don't have the political will to mobilize the resources to make it happen." Fourth, Dr. Gerald Mboowa, winner of the 2020 Anglophone Young Investigator's Award and bioinformatics researcher in Nigeria, suggested that research agendas are imposed by the West since they provide funding and often undercut initiatives that could benefit local communities.

## BE OPTIMISTIC

You catch more flies with honey than with vinegar is ever represented when one looks at health psychology and Black people. Whenever there are discussions about Black people and health in general, the focus is on health disparities, or what is missing. However, an emphasis on health promotion could give us a laundry list of protective behaviors to be encouraged among people of African descent. Deciding to promote health can lead people to focus on the optimal behaviors they may be already exhibiting.

The health psychology research is replete with findings on the relationship between positive affect and optimal outcomes. One such study involving a mostly female African American college sample, as well as a community sample, was conducted by Pierce et al. (2018). A positive correlation between positive affect and life satisfaction was noted in their study. With the community sample, Pierce et al. (2018) collected cortisol activity in their saliva, as a physical way of measuring well-being. The average age of the sample was 31 years and most had experienced post-secondary education. The researchers found low cortisol activation to be associated with high positive affect (PA). In reference to negative affect (NA), they concluded, "Even in the context of high NA, high PA may contribute to well-being . . . on the contrary, when PA is low, well-being may depend upon conjointly low NA" (p. 458).

The emphasis on a strengths perspective in this book takes away from unwarranted comparison. For example, comparing the health attitudes of Black people with the health attitudes of white people turns into a zero-sum game. Fewer white people believe that racism even exists compared to Black, Indigenous, and people of color (BIPOC). The failure to acknowledge racism guarantees an endorsement of a deficit model. Focusing on the health attitudes and behaviors of Black people, without comparing them to white people, gives us a chance to cull optimal behavior that exists despite racism.

In 1976, Jackson wrote about healing using a framework based on African origins. When we use a deficit model of Black health, this is often based in a European framework while a strengths-based model is based in an African framework, according to him. Jackson (1976) also suggested that one's culture must be accepted in order to provide therapy to the person; the same can be said regarding providing physical health treatment to people. He proposed a two-pronged approach to mental health for Black people that both considers their cultural strengths and provides tools for targeting the racism that exists in their lives.

## DON'T BELIEVE THE HYPE

Many studies that do look at the effects of racism among Black people offer incomplete pictures of it. While racism, and internalized racism, speak to the negative effects of these constructs in the lives of people of African descent, racial socialization and optimal racial identity tell the rest of the story by addressing how these variables buffer racism and internalized racism, an extension of racism.

Many researchers have examined the relationship between racial identity and discrimination. For example, in the National Survey of American Life from the early 2000s consisting of African Americans and African Caribbean people, Chae et al. (2011) found that those with high racial identity were less likely to experience psychological distress if they were exposed to racial and non-racial discrimination, compared to those with low racial identity. Most of the sample were poor, employed women and almost half lived in the southern part of the United States.

Racial/cultural identity is not the only piece that promotes healthy behaviors. The rejection of racism is also key. Internalized racism occurs when Black people believe stereotypes about Black people. Researchers examined the relationships among symptoms of anxiety, racist experiences, and internalized racism (Graham et al., 2016). They found that internalized racism mediated the relationship between racist experiences and anxiety. Most of the participants in this study had one to three years of college. The average

age was around 25 and the majority of the sample were women. Experiences with racism were measured by the Schedule of Racist Events. Internalized racism was significantly related to both stress and anxiety symptoms as well as experiences of racism. It also predicted stress and anxiety when the experiences of racism were removed. In other words, internalized racism did the job of racism.

Consequently, it is so important to inoculate Black people against racism. Graham et al. (2016) did note that a limitation of the study was the lack of a scale measuring self-evaluation. So, while Black people will experience racism, the question of one's reaction to this racism is dependent on the amount of racism that has been internalized.

What is interesting about this study is that it included Black participants who were both U.S. born and foreign born. They differed on internalized racism scores. What would you predict? The foreign-born Black people were less likely to have internalized racism, compared to those born in the United States. This shows that another way to promote health among people of African descent is to disrupt the narrative so that young people do not internalize racism and are inoculated against it from a young age.

The relationship between internalized racism and mental health was also examined by Mouzon and McLean (2017). They used data from the National Survey of American Life (early 2000s), examining African American and African Caribbean participants. Mental health was conceptualized by asking questions about depression and serious psychological distress. Internalized racism was assessed with the Stereotypes scale, and they were asked about the extent to which they believed they controlled their lives with a Mastery scale as well as overall physical health status. The average age of African Americans and African Caribbeans born overseas hovered around 42, while the African Caribbeans born in the United States was close to 36 years of age. The health status of most ranged from good to excellent, and most had at least a high school diploma.

The researchers found that internalized racism predicted both depression and serious psychological distress to a lesser degree. Mouzon and McLean (2017) also reported differences in internalized racism scores such that African Caribbeans who were not born in the United States had lower scores and higher mastery scores, compared to African Americans. U.S. born African Caribbean scores fell between these two groups. Furthermore, the relationship between internalized racism and serious psychological distress was moderated by mastery. The higher one's mastery, the lower the effect of internalized racism on serious psychological distress. In other words, the lower one's mastery, the stronger the relationship between internalized racism and psychological distress. This relationship was lowest for non-U.S. born African Caribbeans.

The notion of mastery could be attributed to one's cultural identity although the researchers did not measure this. If a Black person is secure in who they are, then they are likely to exhibit mastery in the face of environmental pressures which may tell them they are unworthy.

While Mouzon and McLean (2017) noted differences in internalized racism, as measured by beliefs in stereotypes, Graham et al. (2016) measured internalized racism with the self-hatred subscale of the cross racial identity scale. Like Mouzon and McLean (2017), however, Graham et al. (2016) also noted differences in internalized racism among their participants. They found that those born outside of the United States had lower scores. It seems that differences in internalized racism among Black people can be attributed to a range of experiences.

The differences existed between being born in the United States where not only is a Black person in the minority, but also they are given messages of inferiority. Racial socialization of children serves to buffer against these messages. For Black people born overseas, the added layer of awareness of racism is necessary to a much lesser degree as they are in the majority. This is not to say that there is no need for racial socialization as majority Black countries may still have skin lightening creams in grocery stores. The insidiousness of racism touches people of African descent around the world; thus, the legacy of colonization necessitates cultural affirmation.

Part of internalizing racism is adopting the ideas of what is considered beautiful in a system of racism. Not only do skin lightening creams represent the primacy of European standards of beauty even in mostly Black spaces, but this also includes engaging in unhealthy eating habits in an effort to be thin. Gilbert et al. (2009) assessed eating disorders among African American, African Caribbean, and African female students at an HBCU (historically Black college/university). They found that internalizing the Western ideas of beauty predicted the drive toward being skinny, bulimia (for African women), and body dissatisfaction among the women.

## RACISM VERSUS INTERNALIZED RACISM VERSUS SELF-HATRED

One of the scales measuring internalized racism, the self-hatred subscale of the Cross-Racial Identity Scale (CRIS) (Worrell et al., 2004) made me consider whether internalized racism is the same as self-hatred. A review of literature exploring self-hatred was conducted by Baldwin (1979). He provided an overview of studies showing that Black children chose white dolls over Black dolls when asked about preferences. For years, this has been presented as evidence of Black self-hatred. However, not only did he report inconsistencies in this research, but he also discussed other studies such as one by Albert Beckham in the *1920s*, finding that most of his 3,000- plus sample of Black people were happy with who they were.

The difference between self-hatred and internalized racism can be explained by the fundamental attribution error. In individualistic cultures or worldviews, behaviors or beliefs are explained by self-hatred, by focusing on the person. For collectivist cultures or worldviews, behaviors or beliefs are explained by internalized racism and the consideration of environmental forces. It might even be said that self-hatred employs the use of a deficit model and internalized racism offers hope for a strength-based model. Baldwin (1979) suggested that the self-hatred paradigm ignored the role of culture.

Because the focus of this book is on optimal health behaviors and beliefs of Black populations, we will use internalized racism as it is indicative of a collectivist worldview which gives us a cultural perspective in line with our examination of health psychology and relationships to people of African descent. Self-hatred lets racism off the hook; however, internalized racism keeps it accountable. As an aside, self-loathing can happen to anyone; however, not everyone will experience internalized racism. Graham et al. (2016) admitted as much when they suggested that the lack of a self-evaluation measure was a limitation of their study which used the CRIS, conceptualizing internalized racism as self-hatred.

Banks and Stephens (2018) suggested that rather than using the term "internalized racism," we should consider using "appropriated racial oppression" as it puts the onus back on the system. They noted that the critique of psychology is always that there is too much emphasis on individual behavior at the expense of collective movement or structural barriers. Going beyond individuality offers a complete picture for health equity to thrive.

## INTERSECTIONALITY

The emphasis on a cultural perspective for viewing health psychology's impact on Black people must include both gender and class. There are certain experiences particular to gender and sexual orientation within and between culture and race. Consequently, an intersectional approach is best for discussing these interrelationships. Many studies about Black people involve poor people, hence the need to note class components as well. This is part of the reason that many assume that Black equals poor. Doing so blinds many to any information that may challenge their beliefs. Airhihenbuwa and Liburd (2006) also suggested that just as gender is socially constructed, reconstructing it toward the promotion of health would be beneficial.

In a lot of ways, class cannot be ignored when discussing people of African descent. Many of the studies I looked at included participants who were on the lower end of the income scale. Middle- and higher-income individuals are in positions which enable them to be less likely to give access to researchers and are more able to protect their respective spaces. People who make less money are more likely to use public services, constantly collecting data and using it to make decisions (or indecisions) about public policy.

I had an experience with class when my older daughter was in high school. The youth risk behavior survey (YRBS) was being given to students at her school, which was classified as a Title I school (and mostly Black and Brown). I found out about it when I happened to visit that day. In the school office, I noticed a couple of people and struck up a conversation. They were from the city's health department and told me they were giving the survey to students. I was surprised to learn this because I had received no notification about it. I went to my daughter's classroom, as she and her classmates were about to answer the questions. I stopped her from completing the survey and asked the teacher why I was not informed. The teacher said that she had forgotten to send the information home with students.

I left the school livid because the other children in my daughter's class were taking the YRBS without their parents' permission. My first call was to the Centers for Disease Control. I spoke with the person overseeing its dissemination. She was concerned when I told her what happened, as she returned my call immediately while on her vacation. My next call was to the city's health department. The person I spoke with assured me that the data from that classroom would be destroyed.

The subsequent call to more affluent school districts in the area told me everything that I suspected. They did not give the YRBS. However, the school district my children were in did; their district explained to me that they give blanket consent and inform the parents by sending a note home. I am not clear to this day whether students gave their assent. However, the YRBS is evidently skewed so that low-income youth are overrepresented, as opposed to middle- and high-income youth. This was over 15 years ago, but one could be curious about whether there is more representation of other income brackets now. Thus, throughout this book because most studies involve low-income populations, in cases where this does not occur, I will note the socioeconomic status of participants in the study.

## THE IMPORTANCE OF CONTEXT

Much psychological research is discussed without the benefit of contextual analysis. This is a mistake in many ways. Due to the lack of a complete picture of history being offered in the K–12 system, too many students misunderstand some previous research as it relates to people of African descent. And we don't know what we don't know. The danger of a single story is a TED Talk by Chimamanda Adichie and for too long psychological research has been offering just that—a single story. For instance, research is still being published from the Flint (Michigan) studies of adolescents; however, there are future implications to be considered in psychological and physical health due to lead contamination through water pollution which occurred within the past ten years. There are whole generations being affected and children realizing at an early age that their lives do not matter. The same has been found in other parts of the world. There are so few studies in Africa that discuss the protective factors associated with optimal health among young people.

It is assumed that Black people in other locales do not place a premium on racial, ethnic, or cultural identity, as they would in the United States. This is evidenced by the lack of measures in much of the health psychology research there. There are so few studies that consider racial, ethnic, or cultural identity measures in African or Caribbean research. It is rare in Canadian or British studies. But it is also possible that in places where Black people are not the minority, identity may not be as important. A clue that this might be the case may be found in segregated populations of the past and present in the United States.

While continental Africans are aware of their ethnicity, Africans in the diaspora are more aware of race and not as clearly connected to their ethnicity, often defined as Spanish speaking in the United States. The cultural piece is connected to both race and ethnicity and it is hard to separate race, culture, and ethnicity. Hence, the terms *racial identity*, *ethnic identity*, and *cultural identity* will be used interchangeably throughout this work; although researchers will identify the measures that they are using to assess an identity in the studies I am discussing.

Migration may also be a variable that makes a difference in health outcomes among Black people. For instance, the percentage of African American and Caribbean English with cardiovascular disease or diabetes were similar, while hypertension percentages were also higher among African American and Caribbean English, compared to Caribbean Americans. This was noted in a study by Nazroo et al. (2007) and may lend credence to the protective factors of culture, which would be compromised in settings where Black people are in the minority if not for intentional racial/ethnic/cultural socialization.

## COMMUNITY MATTERS

The role of the community in promoting health cannot be understated. Johnson and Rodrigues (2016) found that if community members are involved in health initiatives, they are more likely to participate in them in their study in Trinidad and Tobago. The same could be said for community members in diverse locales. They also suggested that health-oriented institutions need to see the strengths that already exist in community and build upon those.

African Caribbean residents of the United Kingdom were interviewed by Campbell et al. (2004) about their perceptions of partnerships of health services. They reported wanting to be involved but the issue of mistrust was a common theme. The participants noted that they were overprescribed and the powers that be did not do a good enough job of empowering them to determine their own destiny. They pointed to a lack of a race focus and cultural concordance as well. It seems only by having community health partnerships based in trust (especially after past failures) can communities thrive (Campbell et al., 2004). The similarity of complaints between the United Kingdom and the United States Black communities is food for thought.

While the Western diet has been exported in many parts of the world, it has been mimicked in the Caribbean as well. Harris et al. (2021) found that the consumption of processed foods such as breads, sodas, and chips in Barbados was on par with the United States among younger people, compared to older people, when the study took place in 2012. On the other hand, an increase in fruit and vegetable intake was promising and the percentage of men who were physically inactive had decreased between 1990 and 2012 in Barbados in a study by Sobers et al. (2019). They also found that cardiovascular disease had decreased in Barbados, largely due to medical interventions during this time, which included pharmaceuticals.

We already know what the deficit model of health psychology indicates but because this book focuses on optimal ways of viewing Black people, let us look at how health appears when we view people of African descent with a progressive lens. This new lens endorses an interdisciplinary approach. The early involvement of sociologists such as Du Bois in health is testament to the need for this approach to health psychology among Black populations, and will be discussed in the second chapter, a brief history.

# Chapter 2

# A Brief Cultural History

The past is unpleasant, so this may be the most challenging chapter in this book; however, there are some bright spots to consider. Black people are not just white people with a different skin color. Focusing on race differences has often overshadowed cultural differences. While many believe that African culture was eliminated due to the impact of slavery, there is not enough evidence to support the belief in its complete breakdown. Black culture is adaptive to environmental conditions with enough remnants of respective African cultures that have survived from generation to generation. Mitchell-Jackson (1983) suggested that the belief that Black people do not have a culture may be why culturally specific therapies are sparse. The same can be extended to how the medical profession treats Black people. They are either mistreated due to skin color or treated due to skin color. The manifestation of the treatment process is grounded in racism.

In the 1972 book *Racism and Psychiatry*, a history of psychiatry's treatment of Black people was outlined by Thomas and Sillen. The problem of challenges in Black mental health being treated as a criminal justice issue were noted then. This continues to this day. Historically, police officers decided whether psychiatric help was warranted and more often than not took a Black person to jail rather than to a mental health facility. The authors mentioned psychiatrist Frantz Fanon as an example of a practitioner-activist and suggested to other psychiatrists at the time that they have "a dual responsibility. [They] must participate in the larger fight against racism . . . [and have] a specific professional responsibility to the Black patient" (Thomas & Sillen, 1972, p. 140). They also noted that "Struggle against racism is stress . . . but it is also healthy." They went further to suggest that anything threatening the existence of one's being should be met with resistance, as this is an optimal way to be. The Black Lives Matter protests of the summer of 2020 were the largest movement in the history of the United States and possibly the world. Doing so in the midst of a pandemic, while stressful, contributed to a new sense of agency discovered by its participants and provided evidence of Thomas and Sillen's assertions.

Health psychology emerged as a field in the 1970s, but it was not until the 1980s that it included an exclusive focus on people of African descent. It was on that of Black women. Prior to 1988, there is a dearth of literature on Africana health psychology, which considered a cultural perspective by including racial and/or ethnic identity factors. These considerations were initially identified in counseling, such as the issues of cross-race therapy sessions. With more research evolving in health psychology, such as the recognition of racial discrimination as a key contributor to psychological distress, the possibility that buffers may be rooted in cultural variables such as racial identity, spirituality, and collectivism, among others, has been promoted.

Historically, three Black identities were suggested by Erikson in 1950 in *Childhood and Society*, which won a national book award. They included (1) "mammy's oral-sensual 'honey-child'—tender, expressive, rhythmical, (2) evil identity of the dirty, anal-sadistic, phallic rapist 'nigger,' and (3) clean, anal-compulsive, restrained friendly but always sad 'White man's Negro'" (p. 213). This conception was mentioned in a case study by Chethik et al. (1967) about two Black children in a mostly white residential treatment facility. They suggested the children's patterns of behavior included their heightened awareness of race, their attempts to blend in (which they considered colorblindness), and the belief that their recovery was related to how less Black they saw themselves.

If the earliest conceptions of Black identity, promulgated by psychologists such as Erikson, were negative, grounded in the 1902 looking glass theory of Cooley, or seen as a manifestation of their perception of their culture, it is no wonder many modern research studies of Black populations do not include culture. If the perception of Black people is that there is nothing good about their culture, then of course there is no consideration of its role in health. Or researchers do consider culture, but its stereotypical aspects are associated with health. It is even possible that they continue to equate race with culture, when the cultural concept of "all my skin folk ain't my kin folk," a nod to Zora Neale Hurston (and a common phrase among Black people), does *not* support the race equals culture notion. So, if one does not have an identity, then wouldn't it follow that one does not have a culture?

We have known for a long time about the relationship between racial identity and psychological well-being. For women, gender identity is an added dimension; but for Black women in a study by Pyant and Yanico (1991), gender identity was related to nothing. Psychological well-being was negatively related to the pre-encounter scale scores (based on Cross's conception of racial identity) for college (average age of 19) and non-college (average

age of 30) female students, most of whom worked full-time. Over 40% were white-collar workers (Pyant & Yanico, 1991).

In so many ways, the past plays a role in health outcomes for Black populations. However, playing a role does not mean that it is the sole determinant of these outcomes. For instance, many media pundits suggested that the reason for vaccine hesitancy among African Americans is due to the Tuskegee experiment. However, I'm not sure where the evidence is that they mention the experiment as the reason for hesitancy. Rather than making assumptions about how Black people treat their health, it is a better idea to ask them instead.

## THE WAY BACK

We can draw a crooked line between the flu pandemic of 1918 and the COVID-19 pandemic. Although the news was inevitably and consistently dire, Krishnan et al. (2020) viewed this from a perspective of resilience, as opposed to using a deficit model. They proposed a way forward by learning the lessons of history. The rumors that "Black people don't get sick" were prevalent then, as they were in the early days of the COVID-19 pandemic, in addition to the "it's just like the flu" mantra. Krishnan et al. (2020) stated, "Perhaps the most important conclusion drawn from an analysis of the 1918 influenza pandemic is that minority communities are resilient, are resourceful, and find restoration in community" (p. 478). While the 1918 flu pandemic provided opportunities for Black nurses to serve in the Red Cross and the Army Nurse Corps, where they had previously been denied due to their skin color (Jones & Saines, 2019), the jury is still out on other opportunities arising due to the COVID-19 pandemic.

People of African descent have always taken care of their own. The legacy of care is what has sustained these communities for centuries, and it has not been abandoned. However, it has been compromised in some situations, largely due to the lure of materialism at the expense of spirituality, a cultural value. Nevertheless, conversations with elderly populations are replete with legacy of care tomes, such as "it takes a village to raise a child."

From a cultural standpoint, consequently, Black people were less likely than others to put their elderly in nursing homes. They were also less likely to send family members to mental health institutions, choosing to struggle instead with them. This is not to say that other groups do not care about their vulnerable, but it is to say that how Black people generally care for their vulnerable is different.

The history of slavery across much of the African diaspora was not enough to break the cultural patterns common across various groups. Those who were scattered were prone to form connections to make a new culture that was an amalgamation of various ethnic groups. The new and existing patterns of health care continued, from the mental (often spiritual) to the physical.

Africans practiced inoculation on the continent. While vaccines historically in the West were initially meant to ensure the survival of enslaved people, Africans brought with them practices for guaranteeing their continued health. The Akreens/Gah were one such ethnic group who inoculated their people (Weaver, 2012). Africans carried with them not only knowledge of inoculation but also use of herbs and roots to treat wounds inflicted by the enslaver. Plant knowledge was expanded among *hospitalières* (mostly enslaved African women) on French plantations, due to new environmental patterns. In the United States, knowledge of inoculation was transmitted from Onesimus, an enslaved person in Boston (Weaver, 2012).

Enslaved African people also practiced a form of medicine to treat other enslaved people on French plantations such as Saint-Domingue, Martinique, Saint-Barthelemy, Grenada, Saint Lucia, and Dominica. Their duties included "bloodletting, childbirth assistance, wound operations, and general healthcare" (Weaver, 2012). Some of the enslaved even made surgical instruments (Weaver, 2012). In St. Croix (U.S. Virgin Islands), there were enslaved women nurses who used herbs and roots to treat other enslaved people (Reifschneider, 2018). The community of care cultural notion is thus evident in the way that it existed on the continent and in the diaspora.

There were also plantation hospitals throughout the Caribbean (Reifschneider, 2018). Remnants of a hospital at Cane Garden still stand (in much the same way that some cabins for the enslaved still stand in the United States). One would be within their rights to say that medical mistrust began with the invasion of white people (as colonialism) and their forcibly removing African people from the continent (as enslavement). The practice of medicine on enslaved people by white doctors was meant to make them dependent on white people for their health.

An aspect of slavery and beyond involved experimentation on Black populations who white doctors believed could tolerate great degrees of pain. For instance, the history of gynecology in the United States is tied to American slavery. Holland (2018) reported about the "father" of American gynecology, J. Marion Sims, who not only conducted a series of experiments with Black women who were enslaved, choosing not to use anesthesia, including Lucy, Betsey, and Anarcha (who had the most surgeries), but also performed surgeries on Black children. His statue was removed from Central Park after years of protests in 2018 (Sayej, 2018). Another doctor who enslaved people, François Prévost, perfected C-sections on enslaved women (Cooper Owens & Fett, 2019). While medical care was provided to ensure physical survival of the enslaved, as well as to experiment on them, the health care *from the enslaved* was based on remnants of culture from the continent. Thus, communities of care became "adaptive and strategic in response to their surrounding circumstances" (Reifschneider, 2018).

## BLACK HISTORY

W. E. B. Du Bois, a sociologist, offered one of the earliest assessments of health among people of African descent in his work, *The Philadelphia Negro,* in 1899. He did not suggest the constant comparisons of Black to white when we know that is like comparing apples to oranges. Rather, he suggested comparing apples to apples when he noted, "In considering the health statistics of the Negroes, we seek first to know their absolute condition, rather than their relative status" (p. 52) in order to understand how it has changed over the years.

Doing so in current health psychology research would give us something very different. Using white people as a model of how health should look is always going to be a mistake due to its failures to consider change within a community. And, as previously stated, disparities in health still mean that those health problems exist.

Du Bois dispelled the myth of the strong enslaved African noting unsanitary conditions and death rates that did not match it. As evidence, he reported that the death rate decreased between 1820 and 1896 for Black people; the obvious reason being the abolition of slavery. Medical mistrust was mentioned due to a lack of kindness from health care professionals if Black people were to go to hospitals, suggesting that they "would almost rather die" (p. 52). He suggested that the way toward optimal health would be clean water, clean air, and clean eating, among other variables.

E. Franklin Frazier also wrote about psychological factors in Black health as a sociologist in 1925. He discussed causes of disease offered by Black people as "God's providence" (or lack thereof). This, too, is an example of the prominent role of spirituality among Black people. The cures for diseases were also discussed, often based in folkways such as nutmeg as a remedy for many diseases.

The psychology of fear was described by Frazier as the driving force for why Black people behaved the way they did in relation to their health. He suggested that psychological terrorism would affect any people's health, as the environmental conditions set the stage for such, and even encouraged it. This consists not only of restrictions for how Black people move but also their abilities to recognize their full potential. Frazier suggested that economically poorer Black people experienced these beliefs about disease and cures in that it did not apply to all Black people. Second, he suggested that Black people in the North had more mental illness because they could not self-actualize. This might be viewed as an extension of beliefs, beginning in the 1840s with census numbers promulgated by John C. Calhoun, senator from South Carolina. Calhoun insisted that Black people in the North had more mental illness because the natural state for African people was to be enslaved; the number of mentally challenged Black people outnumbered the number of Black people in a town in Massachusetts (Whoriskey, 2020).

In a lot of ways, the mental and physical health of Black people has been affected by the social environment, regardless of class status and location. Frazier (1925) ended with "we see a disposition on the part of whites to discount the value of Negro life, and to oppose efforts to reduce infant mortality and increase his resistance to disease" (p. 490). This echoed Du Bois (1899), who stated, "There have . . . been few other cases in history . . . where human suffering has been viewed with such peculiar indifference" (p. 56). It is tragic that we still have these challenges decades later, as seen in the Black Lives Matter movement, born under a Black (biracial) U.S. president.

Early Black doctors connected health to structural variables for people of African descent. Gamble (2016) spotlighted Black women doctors who promoted health equity. Dorothy Boulding Ferebee spearheaded the Mississippi Health Project where treatment of the whole person was involved. She led vaccination efforts against smallpox and diphtheria in the 1930s, in addition to providing health exams. The project lasted for seven years. Virginia Alexander opened a private hospital in north Philadelphia, Aspiranto Health Home, to provide a refuge against pervasive racism. Maternal care and health education were among many services provided to the surrounding community.

The health status of Black people in the United States has its fits and starts attributed to how the government has treated this group. Cornely and Alexander (1939) offered one of the earliest assessments and one wonders about where the United States would be if some of their suggestions were implemented. While the researchers compared the health status of Black people to white people, our focus in line with the tone of this book is on how Black people had progressed up to that point. At that time, they noted that there were not enough Black doctors, which is still the case nearly a century later.

While half of Black people lived in the South; only a third of Black doctors were available in those areas. These were among many disadvantages noted by the researchers, but they also surveyed over 40 public health officials, finding that those areas with more Black people employed in their ranks were more likely to report progress with Black health over previous years (Cornely & Alexander, 1939).

The percentage of Black doctors compared to the percentage of Black people in the United States has not had large changes since 1900. Trends were examined between 1900 and 2018 by Ly (2018). In 1900, Black people were almost 12% of the population but the percentage of Black doctors was under 2%. Fast- forward over 100 years, the percentage of Black people still hovers close to 12% and the percentage of Black doctors is slightly over 5%. Black women doctors are now over 2%.

## PROMOTING HEALTH

The National Health Improvement Week was started by Booker T. Washington in 1915. The Office of Negro Health was founded in the 1920s, the culmination of the involvement of the Public Health Service. At the 15th annual National Negro Health Week, March 31–April 7, 1929, the objective was "A Complete Health Examination for Everybody." There is a drawing of a Black woman holding a basketball on the poster. In a poster commemorating its 25th anniversary, the event was held April 2 through April 9, 1939. The Texas Tuberculosis Association sponsored the poster. The 1939 objective was "the citizen's responsibility for community health." National Negro Health Week and the Office of Negro Health were subsumed in service to integration in 1951.

The role of HBCUs in health promotion has a storied history, seen in Booker T. Washington's establishment of a means to improve health. As the founder of Tuskegee Institute (now University), he could make an impact on the surrounding Black community. Mary McLeod Bethune supported such efforts and further believed that Black people should be represented among researchers into the health about Black people as an integral part of what the U.S. Public Health Service had to offer. W. E. B. Du Bois, too, was concerned about the health of Black people, as a pan- Africanist and a sociologist, having established the sociology department at Atlanta University (now Clark-Atlanta University).

The National Center for Bioethics in Research and Health Care currently exists at Tuskegee. It was established in 1999 after a presidential apology to the men in the Tuskegee Study of Untreated Syphilis in the Negro Male (Warren et al., 2012). The center is guided by Dr. John Chissell's theory of Optimal Health, which will be discussed in the next chapter.

The meaning of biomedical ethics when dealing with people of African descent was elucidated by Toldson and Toldson over 20 years ago. They described how an African identity looked and suggested that Black psychologists spur clients toward an African identity that would play an optimal role not just in their mental health, but also their physical health. They also suggested that if people followed bioethics as related to skin color, then Black people would be more accepting of the melanin in their skin (and less likely to be exposed to dangerous chemicals in lightening cream). Toldson and Toldson (2001) also suggested that informed consent might be a problem in a system in which Black people have minimal power and that the notion could be better conducted by checking with community leaders who would endorse collectivism endemic to Black people.

## CULTURALLY COMPETENT CARE

Culturally competent care is the most effective way of impacting the health of people of African descent. This occurred without question on the continent, during enslavement around the world, and in recovery from both colonialism and slavery. Such a practice would be inherently anti-racist.

Cooper Owens and Fett (2019) suggested as much in their work and outlined two examples of anti-racist health care done right. One was the Black Panther Party's medical outreach to the community. Their free clinics provided a variety of services for mothers and children in particular. The other was Mound Bayou, Mississippi, an all-Black community that provided free health care through its Tufts-Delta Health Center which was federally funded. In both instances, the opportunity to offer medical services to the community were some of the earlier instances of culturally competent care, especially after the cessation of Negro Health Week.

## MEDICAL MISTRUST

The history of medical mistrust by Black people continues not to be history. As recently as the 1990s, Pfizer responded to a meningitis outbreak in Kano in Nigeria. They brought drugs that had not been approved by the U.S. Food and Drug Administration (FDA) but gave them to Nigerian children, 11 of whom consequently died (Garba & Abidakun, 2021). Many became afflicted with speech and hearing problems, paralysis, and blindness. By 2007, the Nigerian government, the state of Kano, and families sued Pfizer for damages. The company said the side effects were due to meningitis, yet they failed to publish their findings about Kano. Pfizer had forged documents indicating Nigerian approval but settled for $75 million without taking responsibility.

Issues around consent were mentioned as well. The medical industry has a past and present of not gaining consent for participants in drug studies, in spite of Pfizer's insistence that they did in this case. On the other hand, Pfizer notes that Nigeria had no IRB equivalent (Garba & Abidakun, 2021). Even if there were no organizations likened to the IRB (Institutional Review Board), Garba and Abidakun (2021) suggested that the Nuremberg Code (1940s) and the Helsinki Declaration (1960s) are supposed to guard against involving people in experiments which may eventually harm them. Multinational corporations continually refuse to abide by these guidelines. The primary reason that we have IRBs in the first place is because of the Tuskegee syphilis experiments where treatment was withheld for hundreds of Black men in order for researchers to examine its long-term effects (LaMorte, 2016).

In another case, HIV drugs were tested on Black and Brown HIV- positive children in New York City. The BBC described what happened in their 2004 documentary *Guinea Pig Kids*. The medicines were making the children ill; some of the side effects included chills, itching, appetite suppression, and organ failure. Caregivers and parents had their children removed by ACS (Administration for Children's Services) for not giving the medication to them. Many of them were subsequently placed in foster care or Catholic children's homes such as Incarnation Children's Center. ACS provided consent for the children, subverting any rights that parents had. Some of the children are buried in mass graves at the home, but their causes of death are listed as natural causes. Foster parents were paid to give the drugs to the children. The parties with stakes in these clinical trials included Columbia Presbyterian Hospital, Merck, GlaxoSmithKlein, and Pfizer.

As you can see, medical mistrust is a key component of health discussions among people of African descent and is rooted in a tenuous past. Morgan (2004) examined conversations about organ donations among the African American participants in her study. She found that those with less knowledge about organ donation had a greater degree of medical mistrust. Unfortunately, due to the low Cronbach alpha of the scale used to assess medical mistrust (normed on a mostly European American sample), this variable was not a major factor in whether African Americans would have discussions about organ donations. However, their conversations with family members predicted favorable attitudes and knowledge about the matter. Masi and Gehlert (2008) also explored medical mistrust, one of many factors examined when they asked African Americans about their experiences with breast cancer treatment through focus group interviews. They found that mistrust of physicians was linked to their ties to the pharmaceutical industry. This is not without merit, as researchers recently noted that doctors get paid for providing chemotherapy drugs (Ellis, 2006).

The idea of Black genocide is not too far-fetched, given the history of enslavement, colonialism, and unwarranted medical experimentation. A study in 1973 explored this notion among Black participants who were asked about their perceptions as related to birth control, exploitive labor, and "militant" views. Turner and Darity (1973) found regional, gender, age, and educational differences in whether they agreed with specific statements in that Black people in the north, men, those younger than 28, and those with fewer years of education were more likely to be fearful of Black genocide.

Researchers have suggested ways to battle medical mistrust. They include at least three proposed by Krishnan et al. (2020). For one, community and media who have a trusted legacy in the community should be partnered with health care workers and institutions. Secondly, the health care system should become so diverse and expansive that it can provide "racially concordant care teams" (p. 478). Doing so would make it easier for Black people to locate Black doctors. Third, medical research should be community-based and participatory in nature. Any research involving Black people should include the input of Black people in its design; this is too often not the case.

Health care providers should at a minimum offer an array of treatment options to their patients. Doing so would encourage trust between the doctor and the patient. A patient knowing and believing that the doctor trusts them to make the right decision for themselves enables that patient to trust the doctor more. Part of what should be considered when we discuss the issue of medical mistrust is the issue of respect. This is what is missing from the conversation. However, Song et al.'s (2012) study contributed to this topic. A few of the breast cancer patients in their study drew a line between respect and trust, reporting on discussions about religious faith. They reported that when their doctors shared their faith, it increased the trust they had in them.

## SELF-DESTRUCTION?

Violence is a public health crisis that affects everyone; health psychology within a cultural context has the potential to tackle those issues as well. Cross (2003) pointed to structural inequalities as the ultimate source of youth violence. He based this on a balanced examination of historical evidence and noted as an example the case of youth in Chicago who had to attend school in shifts and were left to their own devices while their parents worked. He stated that "Blacks exited slavery with the type of social capital . . . that could have readily facilitated their rapid acculturation into the mainstream of American society, had society wanted them" (p. 80). However, I would end this sentence differently. I posit that "Blacks exited slavery with . . . social capital" that evolved as a function of the perpetuation of some African cultural practices. What is more important is not acculturation into the mainstream society in the long run, but both maintaining cultural heritage in the face of daily psychological assaults and being given the opportunity to succeed. I do believe, as Goren (2001) stated, that "the potential power of the community is underutilized" (p. 142).

## BLACK PEOPLE DON'T DO THERAPY

Seeking help for mental health challenges is framed as an issue for the Black community. For years, the belief has been that they do not seek help. However, this may be due to the profession's emphasis on formal methods for obtaining help; it may be more likely that we are ignoring informal methods for getting help. These include talking to family, friends, or even a pastor. It is true, however, that seeking help from mental health professionals is even discouraged among some people of African descent and has been tied to socioeconomic status.

Because of the stigma, the literature is not replete with examples of how this looks among this population. Some of the earlier research includes that by Hendricks and colleagues (1981) who explored help-seeking behavior among 400 African Americans. They found that 36% of them would go to a community mental health center, hotline, or hospital if they were having mental health challenges. A third said they would reach out to informal sources such as friends or clergy. Finally, 31% said they would see someone in the medical profession, like a psychiatrist. The researchers noted class differences in the responses. Access to institutions was preferred by those with less than a high school diploma and blue-collar workers. While women were more likely to reach out if they were experiencing a serious mental health problem, compared to men, men reported seeking help from informal sources to a greater degree than women. It is unclear whether this is still the case; however, the strategies suggested by Krishnan et al. (2020) would be helpful in supporting access to mental health care as well.

## WORK-LIFE BALANCE

We spend so much of our lives working outside of our homes. The environment to which many of us are exposed may be less than ideal. The problem of racist experiences in the workplace among Black people is an added layer to our work lives. Mays et al. (1996), 25 years ago, analyzed data related to this from the National Survey of Black Americans (taken between 1979 and 1980). During the COVID-19 pandemic, many Black workers retreated to their homes to conduct their work. There were anecdotal stories of higher productivity and the ability to focus due to the missing office microaggressions. As states removed restrictions and office workers were called back to their work locations, Black workers have expressed reluctance to go back in because some would be exposing themselves to racist harassment that had ceased for as long as a year.

In a qualitative study of UK (United Kingdom) residents, most of whom were from Jamaica, Higginbottom (2006) asked questions related to their health. The African Caribbean people in her study reported their stress as being related to their employment and attributed their high blood pressure to it. While older participants saw it as a consequence of aging, the younger ones reported being surprised about their diagnosis. Although they experienced hypertension, most of them did not report changing their behavior as a result. Steps toward health equity include providing opportunities for health promotion for those experiencing race- related stress in the workplace.

I could not mention work-life balance without including a discussion of mythical figure John Henry, representing African American men hired to build the railroad in the United States. The legend notes that John Henry beat a steel driving machine in a competition but expired having worked himself to death (National Park Service, n.d.). From this story comes the cultural notion of John Henryism, defined as an "individual's self-perception that he can meet the demands of his environment through hard work and determination" (James et al., 1983, p. 263) extended by James (1994) to explain health outcomes experienced by Black people. While he reported a positive correlation between John Henryism and hypertension among Black men with low education status (James et al., 1983), in later years, researchers found this relationship trended among both men and women of African descent in Nigeria with higher education status (Markovic et al., 1998). This is one of the earlier studies which may provide support to the notion of the "strong Black woman." Furthermore, an inverse association between John Henryism and depression was reported regardless of income group in studies by Robinson and Tobin (2021) and Bronder et al. (2013). However, Hudson et al. (2016) found a positive relationship between the two phenomena among a general sample of African Americans.

The cultural health behaviors among people of African descent will be explained in the next chapter within the context of theoretical perspectives such as John Henryism. Some of these have been used in general research but the need to use theories proposed by people familiar with the culture to explain their behavior cannot be overstated. Models rooted in cultural mores are key to the promotion of health among Black people.

# Chapter 3

# Theoretical Considerations

There are several models and theoretical perspectives guiding research among African-descended populations. Some of them have been proposed by researchers in disciplines other than psychology. They are being grouped dependent on the phenomenon being explained.

A resilience approach is interdisciplinary in nature and involves "overcoming odds, sustaining competence under pressure, and recovering from pressure" (Fraser & Richman, 2001). Going through something may make one more resilient but going through too much might make someone crack under pressure. Rutter (2001) suggested that resilience is not a trait, but a response to specific challenging situations. Resilience is one of many psychological characteristics found to influence health outcomes. For instance, DeNisco (2011) reported that among African American women with type 2 diabetes, their HbA1c levels were low in the face of high resilience.

Another theory that explains an emphasis on healthy behaviors exhibited by African-descended people is the health promotion model. This perspective suggests that there are three components: individual characteristics/experiences, behavior-specific cognitions/affect, and behavioral outcome/health promoting behavior (Pender, 2011). The parts of the theory that would have a collectivist bent include the influence of family, significant others, peers, and health providers as influencers for adopting a health promotive lifestyle. Commitment is also a key factor in that it is dependent on what the individual can gain as well as its strength. Applying this theory to Black populations, one can see that a commitment to one's heritage, with an emphasis on past healthy experiences and *real* models, can predict future healthy practices.

An application of the health promotion model usually compares Black people to other populations and does not seem to capitalize on strengths. This is not to say that the research does not exist but were one to conduct a study based on this model, they would have to ensure a cultural component. The model appears flexible enough to use as an adaptable framework.

Warren et al. (2012) outlined Chissell's theory of optimal health. There are five components: intellectual, emotional, physical, socioeconomic, and spiritual. While the first three could be experienced as optimal intellectual health, optimal emotional health, and optimal physical health and would begin with the individual, optimal socioeconomic health and optimal spiritual health both require collective action. Chissell based his theory on his work with poor Black people over his years in service to the community. Not viewing them through a deficit lens enabled him to develop a model that, if properly communicated, would extend one's life. Doing so enables one to understand that personal responsibility alone is not enough to support optimal health for the masses. As previously mentioned, Chissell's theory is used to drive the research at the bioethics center at Tuskegee.

## CONCEPTIONS OF IDENTITY

Kambon (1992) offered a theory of Black identity, evident in his notion of African self-consciousness (ASC), included as an awareness of spirituality. Recognition of one's African identity/heritage, general philosophy and behavior patterns emphasizing African survival, specific behavior patterns reflecting collective self-affirmation, and resistance against anti-African/ anti-Black forces come together to make up ASC. The African self-extension orientation (ASEO) is the unconscious part of Black identity driving the ASC.

Relationships between cultural identity and health promotion were noted in a study by Thompson and Chambers (2000). They surveyed college students whose average age was 20. The participants completed the African self-consciousness scale, the health consciousness scale, and the health-promoting lifestyle measure. The researchers reported that cultural identity was positively correlated with health responsibility, spiritual growth, and interpersonal relations. These three factors also predicted the promotion of healthy behaviors.

One way of measuring racial/ethnic/cultural identity was developed by Sellers et al. (1998), the multidimensional model of racial identity (MMRI). In it, they proposed four aspects of racial identity: racial salience, racial centrality, racial regard (public and private), and racial ideology (nationalist, oppressed minority, assimilationist, and humanist). They examined meaning and importance of racial identity in their conceptualization. The MMRI is supported by four assumptions: environment influences identity, some identities are more important than others, identity is determined by individual perception, and identity does not occur in stages.

The relationship among cultural identity, pain frequency/severity, and stress among other variables was noted by Bediako et al. (2007). Their sample consisted of sickle cell patients whose average age was 34, almost half of whom had some college but most of whom were not working. They reported a negative correlation between racial identity (conceptualized as racial centrality) and both pain severity as well as use of health care services.

In 1968, Erikson discussed a positive identity with which Black people might have come to the United States. He suggested that the negative identity is fused with stereotypes to determine how Black people treat each other and gave the example of Black people calling each other the n-word. He believed that all ethnic minority groups hate themselves. He also said, "The rate of crime . . . in some Southern counties . . . dropped sharply when the Negro populations became involved in social protest. Unfortunately, a violent society takes nonviolence for weakness and enforces violent solutions" (Erikson, 1968, p. 314). He also suggested that African identity may be a good place to start for Black identity. This would be considered a positive identity and would be land-based (like so many other identities).

Race related stress, experienced as a reaction to a racist event, has been reported among a number of African Americans. However, in a study by Coleman and colleagues (2012), the researchers found that it could be alleviated by one's adherence to their racial/cultural identity. Thus, racial/cultural identity was protective against race related stress. Interestingly enough, they also found that the participants, college students of African descent, who adhered to colorblind ideology also reported lower race-related stress. Coleman et al. (2012) offered that this may be due to their blindness to how racial discrimination looks.

Colorblindness ideology, then, is a double-edged sword. On one hand, its negative relationship to race-related stress works on a temporary basis. On the other hand, endorsing a colorblind ideology may prevent Black people from accepting their African heritage, which has been shown to promote healthy psychological functioning in the long run. The research supporting this, as well as associated statements, is being discussed throughout this book.

## FOCUS ON THE FAMILY

A model proposed by Barbarin (1983) involved coping by Black families and considered environmental impacts. The emphasis on extended family and fictive kin, blended roles/blurred lines between parents, and what psychologists refer to as adultification of children may be best interpreted as children being groomed for their place in the family and having a sense of who they are early as responsibility for others is emphasized. The distinction between individual and family stress is also outlined by Barbarin (1983). He suggested that "family stress is shared" (p. 312), but dependent on whether a person sees themselves as belonging in the first place, as well as their role in the family. For instance, the oldest child may feel financial pressures experienced by the parents that the younger children may not feel. Barbarin's general model in response to stress included the type of stress, how it is interpreted, type of coping, and resources within the family's grasp. The example of childhood cancer is offered as an example in Barbarin's 1983 model.

Another family-based model is the biobehavioral family model (BBFM), conceptualized by Wood (1994). The BBFM suggests that health outcomes are explained using a biopsychosocial perspective and advances the idea that family level factors are related to individual level characteristics such as biobehavioral reactivity and health outcomes. Family level factors include proximity (habits of sharing space/thoughts), generational hierarchy (parenting style), negative parental interaction, triangulation (focus on child or child-parent partnerships), and family responsiveness. The relationship between these two levels (family and individual) is seen as bidirectional. Optimal functioning in this model would involve a balancing act in every factor at both the family and individual levels.

A study by Priest et al. (2020) used this model involving African Americans over the age of 50. Mental health was assessed with one question. Discrimination over one's lifetime and on a daily basis was measured as well as its impact. They found that biobehavioral reactivity mediated the relationship between family support and disease activity. Additionally, while family support was negatively correlated with biobehavioral activity, biobehavioral activity was positively correlated with disease activity. This study's findings show that including a possible protective factor yields results that enable us to focus on promoting those variables. While racial discrimination did not have a direct influence on disease activity, it worked through family support so that racial discrimination and family support were negatively correlated (Priest et al., 2020). As an aside, racial discrimination was positively related to partner and family strain. The researchers made a compelling case for including discrimination when discussing health outcomes for African-descended populations (Priest et al., 2020).

The PEN-3 cultural model was developed by Airhihenbuwa in 1989. It consists of three components: cultural identity (where an intervention could be targeted to a person, extended family, and neighborhood), cultural empowerment (positive, existential, or negative ways that behaviors influence health), and relationships/expectations (perceptions, enablers, and nurturers impacting behavior). The elements overlap in common spaces and are designed to explain behavior in cultural context (Iwelunmor et al., 2010).

The PEN-3 model has been seen in many studies. One involved interviewing mothers in Nigeria about their children's malaria (febrile illness). The cultural empowerment dimension explained the responses given to the researchers. The average age of the mothers was 30, and more than half of them had secondary education or more. They gave positive responses believing their children would get better because they went to the clinic. The participants were also asked about the cause of malaria in their children; a third believed that it came from teething (an example of an existential notion). An example of the negative aspect of cultural empowerment was seen in over half of the mothers who downplayed their children's illnesses. Iwelunmor et al. (2010) noted that positive responses were due to the type of treatment provided by the clinic and its doctors.

Another research study using the PEN-3 model was conducted by DeJesus et al. (2015). They interviewed East African immigrant women living in Washington, DC, about decisions related to HIV testing and reported that cultural practices determined their behaviors and perceptions. The women ranged in age from 20 to 49; most were employed. The researchers' results lend credence to the importance of culture in health promotion. They noted that many models of health assume that people are able to make individual decisions with no regard for the community of whom they are a part. Thus, not only do explanations for the best way forward to optimal health not consider culture, but those assumptions are also steeped in individualist rather than collectivist perspectives.

Public Health Critical Race (PHCR) praxis was proposed by Ford and Airhihenbuwa (2010) as a way to do research in public health so that movement toward health equity is emphasized. The ten principles are race consciousness, primacy of racialization, race as social construct, ordinariness of racism, structural determinism, social construction of knowledge, critical approaches, intersectionality, disciplinary self-critique, and voice. The researchers noted that PHCR is the application of Critical Race Theory to the field of health, as nods to Kimberlé Crenshaw and Derrick Bell.

## SOCIALIZING INFLUENCES

By including a discussion of racial socialization and racial/ethnic/cultural identity in the context of health psychology and Africana populations, we contribute to giving agency to them. Unfortunately, many researchers do not consider the role of racial socialization when studying people of African descent, contributing to further perpetuation of the deficit model embodied by health disparities explorations. Leaving out such vital information hinders our seeing these communities as having an inherent strength.

Racial socialization involves the way that Black parents rear their children to prepare them for the real world. It consists of four parts: cultural socialization, preparation for bias, promotion of mistrust, and silence about race. Caregivers convey these messages by what they say and what they do (Anderson & Stevenson, 2019). Racial socialization's inclusion of cultural transmission is based on the fact that children are impressionable and can be molded. The assumption that racism is part of the global fabric is another. Finally, what is important to one group of Black people may not have the same meaning for another (Stevenson, 1994). For example, African-descended people raised in the southern part of the United States may feel differently about cultural symbols, compared to those African Caribbeans or Africans who immigrated to the United States.

The buffering effects of racial socialization against racial discrimination have been noted. The Racial Encounter Coping Appraisal and Socialization Theory (RECAST) was suggested as an explanation for how racial socialization could mitigate the effects of race-related stress by Stevenson (Anderson & Stevenson, 2019). An intervention based on this, EMBRace (*e*ngaging, *m*anaging, and *b*onding through race), was provided to racially diverse clinicians and African American families to handle trauma associated with seeing media loops of Black people being abused or killed by state actors. The program consisted of racial socialization, racial coping (including stress management), and delivery (such as affection or protection) and was meant to provide an environment conducive to buffering effects of racial discrimination by enhancing optimal family processes (Anderson et al., 2018). There were 20 participants, mostly mothers (one father) and their children ranging in age from 10 to 14. The 15 clinicians involved reported positive feedback about the program while the youth participants reported being better able to communicate their feelings and to relax; parent responses were similar to their children's responses.

Racial socialization was examined among Black youth by Davis and Stevenson (2006). The participants were mostly girls with an average age of 15. They were asked about the social support available to them as well as their symptoms of depression. The researchers found that mainstream socialization was positively correlated to low energy and depression. Failure to see their surroundings as sources of social capital also garnered negative outcomes.

Psychological functioning has been found to be related to racial socialization as well. Barr and Neville (2014) also reported parents racially socializing children to embrace mainstream values predicted less than optimal mental health, similar to Davis and Stevenson (2006). When colorblind attitudes were considered among the 18–22-year-old, multiethnic Black college students, those who strongly endorsed these attitudes experienced more challenges with their mental health if they received the mainstream messages, compared to those with low endorsement of colorblind attitudes.

The insidiousness of colorblindness cannot be understated. It fails to recognize the full humanity of African-descended populations and ignores their culture, race, and ethnicity. Thomas and Sillen (1972) tackled this notion, saying that it divorced Black people from their lived realities and historical impacts, and "to gloss over race in a racist society may in itself be a capitulation to racism" (p. 143).

One theory that would explain overall health prospects of African-descended populations is the PVEST. The Phenomenological Variant of Ecological Systems Theory (PVEST) was proposed by Margaret Beale Spencer (Swanson et al., 2002). It suggests that we cannot talk about development of children in marginalized groups without considering the racist contexts many of them experience and explains the interaction between context and identity. There are five components which include (1) net vulnerability level (ranging from risk to protective factors); (2) net stress level (consists of challenges and social supports); (3) reactive coping strategies (can range from adaptive to maladaptive); (4) emergent identities (ranging from negative to positive stable coping responses); and (5) life-stage coping outcome (from productive to unproductive; Swanson et al., 2002).

The role of the PVEST in racial identity holds promise for future health promotion research among Black youth. Considering their experiences and the impact of the environment in their lives would bring the PVEST to bear and provide optimal ways of being for youth.

The cognitive cultural model was proposed by Whaley (2003) to explain how Black adolescents understand themselves. There are three elements to it: the individual self, the cultural self, and (behaviors contributing to) social roles. Balancing the individual and cultural selves would result in social roles ideally contributing to the greater good. It should be noted that the cultural self would ideally be a consequence of racial socialization based on healthy notions of being Black.

The cognitive cultural model in action was reported by Whaley and McQueen (2020). Mostly Black boys whose average age was 16 were enrolled in the Imani Rites of Passage program and were compared to a control group on measures of racial identity, racial socialization, and violence risk, among other variables. Racial identity and social roles (conceptualized as academic competence and peer social acceptance) increased as a result of participating in the program, endorsing part of the cognitive cultural model.

## RELIGIOSITY/SPIRITUALITY

Spirituality continues to be a key piece to resilience among Africana populations. Consequently, it is not unusual for Black people to seek help from their respective pastors or religious leaders. In response to this, more than a few ministers have undertaken coursework and even earned degrees in the counseling profession. For many African-descended people, faith is so important that they would consider not only seeing their minister but also going to a counselor who matches their religious orientation.

It is useful today to use the word *spirituality* rather than *religiosity*. The numbers of Black people going to church has dropped precipitously since the 1980s. That does not mean, however, that African-descended populations are less interested in embracing a spiritual life. Seeing the stressor as something the universe or the Creator allowed enables one to draw on their strength. The serenity prayer is the best way to describe these types of coping strategies. While Black families cannot control racial discrimination in the health care system, they will use autonomy to determine who interacts with them and treats them respectfully. The extended nature of the Black family allows resource availability not as accessible to some nuclear families.

The influence of spirituality is often seen in health outcomes. For example, a study by Clark and colleagues (2018) reported such a relationship in their longitudinal study of African Americans whose average age was 58. The researchers measured not only religious involvement (beliefs and behaviors) but also spiritual health locus of control, consisting of active (belief that one should be proactive over one's health outcomes) and passive (belief that only God can regulate one's health outcomes) components. Participants' religious actions were related to more fruit intake and likelihood of men taking a PSA test. Both religious beliefs and passive spiritual health locus of control were associated with less binge-drinking.

## INTERSECTIONALITY

Intersectionality as a theoretical framework posits that people experience their worlds in a number of different ways. For instance, Black women would interpret their lives through the lens of race and sex, as well as other variables simultaneously. We should add the layer of class due to their understanding of themselves as well. Because it is nearly impossible to parse out whether someone is treated due to race, class, or gender, we should also consider sexual orientation for some Black women. Intersectionality is usually applied to the experiences of Black women (Collins, 1990; Crenshaw, 1989). Crenshaw's version of intersectionality is based on episodes of oppression, while Collins's version is based on life experiences in general, both positive and negative. It is evident through the "ongoing interplay between Black women's oppression and Black women's activism" (Collins, 1990, p. 237).

The application of intersectionality related to health outcomes was explored in a study by Lewis et al. (2017). They reported negative correlations between gendered racial microaggressions, and both physical and mental health. The relationship between physical health and mental health was positively associated, as well as that of spirituality and social support, and spirituality and gendered racial identity centrality. Gendered racial microaggressions predicted mental and physical health. In other words, the intersectional experience of microaggressions meant one would experience less than optimal physical and mental health (Lewis et al., 2017). The women in this study were a diverse sample of Black people including those with African, Caribbean, and biracial backgrounds with ages ranging from 18 to 78; 13% of them were part of the LGBTQIA (lesbian, gay, bisexual, transgender, queer, intersex, asexual) community, and most had graduate degrees.

## RACE-RELATED TRAUMA AND PTG

Race-related traumas have been experienced by African people around the world. They range from wholesale taking of land in many parts of Africa, such as Namibia and Zimbabwe, to genocides of people who refused to comply. The Maafa or African holocaust resulted in the enslavement of Black people from the United States to South America to the Caribbean. Within the past two years, we have seen Africans evicted from their apartments in China due to COVID-19 fears as well as Africans turned away from borders trying to escape bombings in Ukraine.

The lack of reparations for any of these atrocities only feed this trauma. In the United States, the institutionalization of racism to uphold a system in which Black people are consistently on the bottom perpetuates race-related trauma. We see this in how structures such as those seen in policing, health, political, legal, and economic systems, among others, require a scapegoat in order to survive.

While race-related trauma is one of many experiences felt by Black people, the notion of post-traumatic growth (PTG) also needs to be considered. Manove et al. (2019) discussed their findings regarding this concept among Black women who described what they went through as a result of Hurricane Katrina. Their mixed-method study asked questions of women with high school diplomas (average age of 31) who had household incomes below the poverty level. Most of the women (who had one to five children) were married or had a significant other. Post- traumatic growth was measured with the PTG inventory (PTGI). Most of the women reported that they were able to assess new opportunities as a result of the hurricane. Nearly 40% of them felt closer and grew more compassionate and connected to others. Almost a third experienced an increase in their faith. Relating to others, a facet of PTG, can be considered the collectivism often experienced by Black people. The score on the PTGI subscale "relating to others" was significantly correlated with how participants responded (Manove et al., 2019). It was the only subscale that reflected the interviews that were conducted.

Post-traumatic growth may explain how Black people continue to thrive in the face of challenging odds. This is evident in the previously mentioned study with the Hurricane Katrina survivors, but was also found with Black women who were survivors of intimate partner violence (IPV). Mushonga et al. (2021) interviewed eight women whose average age was 33; they were living in a domestic violence shelter. Most of their social support came from their families and their churches. One of the common themes reported, spirituality, is not surprising considering their reliance on the church by at least half of the women in the study. Other themes they found included motherhood, gratitude, prudence, solitude, and selective attention. The researchers saw prudence, solitude, and selective attention as avoidant, but suggested they also seemed to play a role in PTG. They translated PTG aspects of greater appreciation of life as gratitude, spiritual change as spirituality, and relating to others as motherhood; all of them were emblematic of personal strength.

This overview of theoretical perspectives is not an exhaustive list. As we will see in the next chapter, there are a variety of ways to explain the health behavior of people of African descent.

# Chapter 4

# Moving toward Healthy Living

Can you have positive health outcomes despite experiences with racism? That question has been answered successfully in research studies. The belief, from a protective factors/strengths-based perspective, would be yes. Using a deficit-based model, the answer would be no. Because this book focuses on how African-descended populations can thrive in spite of racism, let us delve into how some of the studies tackled this issue.

There are many variables associated with health promotion. Cultural identity is a key component and is a protective factor against destructive behaviors. For example, Stock et al. (2011) examined how this works among young African American adults. In their first study, the average age of the participants was 18. They found that the stronger one's racial identity, the less likely they were to use drugs; there was a negative correlation between the two variables. In their second study, the average age hovered around 21 years. The feeling of belonging was negatively related to perceived discrimination and positively correlated with self-esteem. Racial identity (affirmation) impacted high users so that they were less inclined to use drugs. In another study, Banks et al. (2021) reported in their sample of mostly young adults whose average age was 23 that racial identity (affirmation) was negatively correlated with both alcohol and cannabis use. In other words, if the participants felt positively about their racial group, it was linked to being less likely to use alcohol and cannabis simultaneously. The researchers reported this finding among a community sample. This may be instructive for college populations as well, many of whom self-medicate. Finally, researchers reported an inverse relationship between cultural identity and psychological distress among African Canadian college students (mostly women) in a study by Smith and Lalonde (2003).

Other researchers, such as Johnson (2002), discussed this relationship among participants whose average age was 37 and about evenly divided between men and women. Most of them were partnered and had completed at least some college. Racial identity was based on Cross' stages; those in the pre-encounter and immersion stages were less likely to engage in health promoting behaviors. However, a positive correlation existed between the internalization stage and health promoting behaviors.

Racial socialization, previously mentioned in an earlier chapter, sets the stage for racial identity among African-descended people. It can serve as a proxy for protecting against less-than-optimal health behaviors. For instance, Brody et al. (2012) found that racial socialization, among other factors, protected against substance abuse for Black youth whose average age was almost 18. The participants who were racially socialized were less likely to abuse drugs. In a related study, researchers examined ethnic identity among African American and Caribbean American college students and found that it was negatively correlated with alcohol and drug use (Heads et al., 2018); it also predicted alcohol use among mostly women whose average age was 20.

## SPIRITUALITY/RELIGIOSITY

The role of spirituality or religiosity in promoting health has been well documented. Spirituality's importance among people of African descent does not just apply to psychological health but also physical health. A discussion of religiosity or spirituality should include mindfulness as a mental health strategy; however, it has not been studied extensively in African-descended populations. Masuda et al. (2009) looked at this among Black college students. They found that mindfulness ("awareness of thoughts, feelings, and sensations," Masuda et al., 2009, p. 115) was negatively related to emotional distress and positively related to psychological flexibility. In other words, those who practiced mindfulness were less distressed and more flexible in their mindsets.

Spirituality's relationship with mental health cannot be understated. In a research study, a sample of mostly female college students at HBCUs and PWIs, both traditional and non-traditional students, reported on their mental health (Mushonga & Henneberger, 2019). Positive mental health was positively correlated with spirituality and social support. There were significant differences on social support between the traditional and non-traditional groups, in that the non-traditional group had more optimal mental health outcomes. Other research in which spirituality was conceptualized as spiritual well-being played a significant role among African American women who had experienced intimate partner violence. With an average age of 35, their substance use and PTSD symptoms were negatively correlated with spirituality (Bliss et al., 2008).

As a cultural value, spirituality should be enhanced among people of African descent. It can protect against negative feelings, such as hopelessness.

One study noted the relationship between these two variables. Among African American and African Caribbean samples, Robinson et al. (2020) found that the higher their spirituality, the lower their hopelessness. The average age of the participants was 42, and most of them had completed high school. Those with chronic diseases and health issues experienced more hopelessness than those without.

Religiosity is a common theme among Black college students. Turner-Musa and Wilson (2006) asked questions related to intrinsic/extrinsic religiosity, social support, and health promoting behaviors of mostly women at an HBCU. They found that those experiencing high levels of both social support and religiosity were most likely to embrace healthy behaviors.

## MAKING MOVES

In line with past health promotion activities, HBCUs usually require classes related to health and/or physical exercise. Ajibade (2011) examined physical activity of African American female students enrolled at an HBCU. She found that those who lived on campus were more likely to exercise compared to those who lived off campus. This speaks to protective features of the campus environment and their investment in campus resources, according to the research.

For many people, it is easier to get moving when one has a group of people with whom to exercise. Li et al. (2012) explored physical activity among Black adults whose average age was 41. The addition of self-efficacy to this health behavior allowed this study to stand out, in addition to social support. The researchers found that social support affected self-efficacy which indirectly affected leisure time physical activity. Perceived neighborhood quality was not related to whether the participants exercised, contrary to how some believe that environmental constraints keep African-descended people from participating in physical activity.

The relationship between racial discrimination and healthy behaviors has been noted in some studies. For instance, racial discrimination predicted cigarette use and physical exercise, paradoxically, in a study by Corral and Landrine (2012). They suggested that their participants, ranging in age from 18 to 95, may have been handling race-related stress by exercising (a positive coping mechanism) and smoking (a negative coping mechanism).

## HARM REDUCTION

Harm reduction is a component of health promotion. Sometimes, people will engage in negative behaviors despite efforts by health educators. An early example of harm reduction in health was methadone clinics for those addicted to heroin. The belief is that eventually people would leave the heroin behind as the methadone was intended to help with withdrawal symptoms. Some researchers would recommend a decrease in drinking behavior in service to harm reduction, as opposed to complete cessation of drinking alcohol, recommended by Alcoholics Anonymous. Needle exchange programs also provide examples of harm reduction; they have decreased HIV risk due to clean needle availability.

African Americans and African Caribbeans were surveyed about their drinking in a study by Herd and Grube (1996). They found that consumption of "Black popular media" was related to more drinking behavior while "Black sociopolitical awareness" and "Black social networks" (which included church attendance) were related to less drinking. Although dated, harm reduction based on the results of this study might involve an increase in social networks which would be in line with cultural values of collectivism.

The story of Fauziya Kassindja told in her autobiography *Do They Hear You When You Cry* and Alice Walker's *Possessing the Secret of Joy* both tackle the challenges of female genital mutilation (FGM). Although this is considered a cultural practice, it has harmed girls in the name of culture. Over the years, there has been movement toward reducing its harm. Women in Senegal and the Gambia were asked about FGM in a study by Shell-Duncan et al. (2018). The researchers reported differences between older and younger women regarding their perceptions of conformity to it in their focus group interviews. Although all the women reported that FGM occurred due to honoring ancestors and out of respect for elders, women over 30 reported being open to change to it, if not seeing it disappear altogether. As a side note, although Senegal has banned FGM, it still occurs in rural areas.

## BUFFERING "ISMS"

Racism in the health care system is a consistent barrier to access, particularly in Western societies. However, not too many studies examine how Black people resist these challenges, as the role of racial discrimination in health outcomes cannot be taken lightly. Because we know that racial discrimination is related to negative health outcomes, by focusing on how to buffer its effects which include emphasizing the role of culture, we can talk about this relationship using a strengths perspective. In a study examining the extent to which racial identity or spirituality buffered against racial discrimination in which participants' average age was close to 32, and mostly single Black women with some college, Drolet and Lucas (2020) reported that those with high racial identity (centrality) had lower C-reactive protein (CRP) when spirituality was high if participants experienced elevated instances of racial discrimination. Cardiovascular disease is often assessed by measuring CRP, which is in the blood. The opposite was found for those experiencing low racism; CRP rose as intensity increased.

The negative impact of discrimination on the health of African-descended people has been a consistent finding among researchers. For example, a study by Christie-Mizell et al. (2017) reported that lifetime discrimination predicted African Americans' and Caribbean Americans' low ratings of their health. When closeness to other Black people was considered, however, the higher their closeness, the higher their ratings of health, in the face of low or high lifetime discrimination. This pattern was not found for Caribbean Americans experiencing low discrimination over a lifetime. For them, low ratings of health were associated with high closeness to other Black people (Christie-Mizell et al., 2017). Another study by Lee et al. (2020) found that cultural identity was negatively correlated with psychological stress, which was positively associated with later racial discrimination. The participants were followed longitudinally as they aged from 20 to 30.

One study found that Black middle-class men were more likely to experience health challenges, and researchers questioned why that might be the case (Hudson et al., 2012). They had advantages that men with lower incomes did not have, but their health outcomes appeared to be similar. The underlying component as to why this might be the case is racial discrimination. For men with lower incomes, structural racism complicating access to adequate health care explains their health outcomes. For middle- class men, they may be more likely to find themselves in integrated settings consisting of racial microaggressions or racial hassles. The outcomes would be similar, consequently, also due to racial discrimination but not due to lack of access.

A prime example of this conundrum would be the case study by Holmes and Heckel (1970) of the first Black male student at a university in the South. He chose to seek counseling services due to his depression and anxiety, evidenced by his chain smoking. It is unclear if he did this as a student at the HBCU from which he transferred. However, a clue that this may not have been a possibility was his reporting feeling stress-free while playing in a band with other Black people at a Black club.

The student talked about feeling like the invisible man and being ostracized by the other students both on campus and in the dorms. The role model persona required his overachievement, in his opinion, and this seemed to be weighing on him as well. In the final stages of therapy, he mentioned his religiosity and search for spirituality. Once again, the theme of spirituality is a constant as well as the collectivism of other Black students on campus. Although he remarked that his paving the way made things easier for others to attend the college who came in after him, he felt estranged from them.

In this case study, he mentioned the Black middle-class preoccupation with imitating white people, as a product of it. This was telling for several reasons. For one, the stress of imitation would lead to negative health outcomes. Second, this may be one of many reasons that some health professionals do not see Black people as having a culture.

Racial discrimination has a different relationship to depression compared to racial identity. The relationship between racial discrimination and depression was strongly and positively correlated for Black college students who embraced an integrationist perspective of racial identity, compared to those with other racial identity perspectives in a study by Banks and Kohn-Wood (2007). Two-thirds of the sample consisted of women who were mostly 18–20 years of age. Furthermore, the relationship between racial identity and depression was also noted in a study by Settles et al. (2010). The average age of the women was 33, and most of them had some college. They reported negative relationships between those two variables.

The recognition of systemic racism, in addition to an emphasis on dismantling it, are issues that accompany race-related trauma. Aymer (2016) reported treating trauma in therapy using ideas from critical race theory. The case study he used was that of an adolescent boy who was a victim of the New York City Police Department's institutional policy of stop and frisk. The therapist and client were able to connect due to their shared experiences of being targeted without cause. The key to his healing was understanding that environmental forces affected his existence, which went beyond his being or behavior.

Treatment of African-descended populations by the larger society can lead to internalizing messages, which sometimes turns into appropriation of racism. If more Black people can acknowledge how larger society treats them, compared to treatment by friends and family, the perspective on race-related trauma might have a less significant effect on them. Aymer (2016) suggested the benefits of going beyond a single story (a nod to Chimamanda Adichie's TED Talk). Encouraging a change in perspective, recognizing the existence of race-related trauma and its affiliated pain, and not viewing Black boys and men through a deficit lens would make all the difference in the world.

LGBTQIA populations are usually not represented in much of the research about Black people. However, they, too, as sexual minorities experience discrimination from many sides and it, too, is an intersectional experience. English et al. (2020) examined this in their study of Black men who have sex with men (MSM). They asked about their feelings as Black men, self-efficacy, psychological stress, and connectedness to the gay community, among other measures. The average age of the participants was 30, and the researchers found negative correlations between positive notions of being a Black man and psychological distress. Positive correlations were noted between gay community connectedness and self-efficacy, and positive notions of being a Black man, and both self-efficacy and emotional awareness. Favorable ideas about being a Black man were associated with being more likely to behave in sexually protective ways. English et al. (2020) noted, "Thus, examining positives at the intersection of race and gender may be critical to future health promotion with Black men who have sex with men" (p. 227).

In one study, Black male South Africans were asked about their cultural identity and condom use. The average age was 21 and most had finished high school; they were from a variety of ethnic groups (Nyembezi et al., 2014). The researchers noted that cultural affiliation was associated with correct and consistent condom use. They also reported that culturally the men would be responsible for any pregnancy, which worked in conjunction with cultural norms from their respective ethnic groups.

## SOCIAL SUPPORT

The role of social support in healthy living cannot be underestimated. The words of our friends and family impact how we take care of ourselves and each other. Fifty-two African American women participated in focus group interviews about prostate cancer screenings and their partners. Allen et al. (2018) reported common themes discussed among the participants who made encouraging, action-oriented comments in the form of providing informational support. They also offered emotional support by praying, making doctor's appointments, and attending doctor's appointments with their partners.

Part of moving toward health also includes those with potentially deadly diseases. For many Black women, HIV disproportionately affects them. Yet, how they live after the diagnosis and continue to take care of their health is sometimes not considered. Dale and Safren (2018) interviewed women living with HIV (average age of 46 years) about their experiences with resilience. Recognizing the importance of community support, they also interviewed community stakeholders. The researchers found that the women coped by drawing on social support which fed their resilience. This resilience came from family members (such as children and grandchildren), romantic partners, friends, and the community at large. The concept of the village was important, not just to the women, but also the community stakeholders. All worked together to reduce the stigma of HIV. It goes without saying that

HIV- positive women leaned on each other for social support as well. Racial discrimination and HIV-related discrimination were mitigated with the resilience emanating from those many sources.

The idea of gaining resilience from social capital is one that does not get enough attention in the health psychology research, particularly as it pertains to African-descended people. The concept of the village is a very important cultural concept thus it makes sense for resilience to also come from others, going beyond individualistic notions of resilience. This is in line with collectivism as a cultural value.

For too many Black women, however, adopting the strong Black woman persona has been adaptive but comes with negative side effects. The strong Black woman model is the belief to which women of African descent see themselves as self-reliant, in control of their emotions, and always willing to help. Thoughts about endorsing a strong Black woman schema, depression, and coping mechanisms were assessed by Jones et al. (2021). They found that adopting this schema was positively correlated with depression and disengagement. Moving toward optimal health outcomes requires women to shed the strong Black woman persona.

One way to mitigate that persona is by leaning into the community of care concept so that it applies to oneself; another way to look at self-care. Taking a timed nap every day is a form of self-care; its importance is often minimized. Not only does sleep affect our mental health but it also affects our physical health. Jerald et al. (2017) found that self-care (which included sleep) was negatively correlated with the depression, anxiety, and hostility in their study with college women whose average age was 22; a small percentage were Afro-Latina.

Moving toward healthy outcomes differs depending on the types of cancer that have been survived. Black breast cancer survivors have been found to have better mental health outcomes compared to those survivors of other types of cancer in a study by Claridy et al. (2018). They also included women who did not have cancer and asked about their physical health; all the women were over 35. The physical health of women without cancer and breast cancer survivors was comparable. The researchers suggested that Black women who were survivors of other cancers need to be supported in their physical and mental health as it seems that breast cancer survivors had more social capital from which to draw support.

## OPTIMIZING DIETS

Part of the legacy of slavery appears in the diets of people of African descent. Those on the continent were most able to hold on to their food origins, although they are being influenced by Western diets such as fast food that is being exported. There is a lot of conversation about food deserts in Black communities. The assumption is that people in these communities only buy food in those communities. However, researchers sometimes make little of the adaptability of Black populations. Rose (2011) reported about such in his study in which 47 participants from two neighborhoods in Detroit were interviewed. He found that they could access fresh foods by grocery shopping at places which were better maintained and stocked. Only 11% of the participants limited their grocery shopping to the surrounding community; a larger percentage (19%) only shopped outside of their neighborhoods.

There are some options available for residents of communities with limited grocery shopping choices. Rose (2011) mentioned the expansion of community gardening programs and the implementation of community non-profit run grocery stores. One example of a non-profit community run grocery store is the Carver Market in South Atlanta. Examples of community gardens abound across the United States as well.

Africans have been in Nova Scotia for centuries and they have managed to hold on to their cultural practices, which include nutritional beliefs. Beagan and Chapman (2012) conducted a qualitative study with them. The 38 participants interviewed ranged in age from 13 to 71 and came from 13 families. How they cooked and ate was discussed, as the participants noted the relationship between food and health. One indication of the community of care and collectivism involved their eating most meals together and shying away from processed foods and restaurants. One of the participants talked about love in the food and it reminded me of one of my aunts talking about cooking food with love.

Cultural notions of food cannot be devalued. Beagen and Chapman (2012) discussed these findings among African Nova Scotian participants in their study as well. Food symbolized both culture and defiance of racism. Cultural mistrust related to health appeared in some of the responses. They included using the term *thick* in reference to being healthy, being skinny as a sign of sickness, and cooking healthy as being considered white because it did not consider African culture. In a related study, ethnic identity (search) was negatively correlated to attitudes toward eating disorders in a study among African American college women, whose average age was 20 (Henrickson et al., 2010).

The assumption that Black women who are overweight do not exercise or eat healthy was laid to rest in research by Alvarado et al. (2015). In their qualitative work involving African Caribbean women in Barbados, most of whom had post-secondary education with an average age of 30, they reported that social support and walking or dancing made it easy to participate in physical activity, as well as positive affect, a motivator. Once again, the issue of social support is key; however, the participants did not see a connection between physical activity and health because there were people that they knew who did everything right but still developed diseases such as diabetes.

It might be a good idea to promote collective action of exercise in an effort to affect health as an indirect way of impacting health. For instance, we see such activities in organizations like Black Girls Run. The women in the Alvarado et al. (2015) investigation felt more comfortable exercising with other women. Nutrition was also discussed, especially in cases where they could not exercise. I have found that this seems to be an acceptable substitute but should not be endorsed as a sole way to stay healthy.

## DECREASING STRESS

Spirituality, spirit, and religion are related to reduction of stress. In a study by Lewis et al. (2021), these three concepts are different, but related. The researchers asked 18 Black college students, mostly women whose average age was 31, about how they used spirit when handling stress; two of the participants were part of the LGBTQIA community. They found that the participants reported themes related to spirit such as engaging in "prayer/spiritual behavior" and "thoughts of asking God for help" in response to stress, among other variables. Participants also reported that connection with the supernatural, belief in/search for God, and connection to God as being in common with spirituality and religion. Lewis et al. (2021) gave me pause when they stated, "It may be more culturally responsive to understand behavioral, affective, and cognitive forms of spirit-reliant responses to stress" (p. 529).

Sometimes stress can spur a person toward action. In one study, race-related stress was found to be positively related to activism among mostly middle-class women whose average age was 27 (Prosper et al., 2021). The researchers reported that spirituality was positively related to activism, specifically, the extent to which one searches for answers to their questions. It should be noted that religious fundamentalism was not related to activism. In many ways, this study reflects the role of spirituality in previous iterations of civil rights movements.

One of the most effective ways to address race-related stress, outside of psychological help, is a basic racial socialization of children in African-descended populations. However, this can occur at any point during adulthood. Jones et al. (2020) explored how coping with race-related stress could look across one's life span. The researchers suggested drawing on the strength of those who have come before us, to heal from race-related stress. In another study, there was no relationship between race-related stress and perceived health. However, when it was combined with difficulties in emotion regulation and anxiety, then perceived health was impacted (Carter & Walker, 2014). The researchers found this among African Americans (about evenly divided between men and women) whose average age was 34.

The United States is at the point where many who are in clinical practice are overwhelmed by the number of clients seeking therapy, not just due to COVID-19, but also due to disturbing loops of Black death. The notion of culture as a proverbial balm of Gilead is not touted enough by psychologists. Jones et al. (2020) suggested that doing so would be a work-around for the cultural mistrust often seen among people of African descent.

We spend most of our lives at work. In our employment, we may experience discrimination. The relationship between perceived discrimination and psychological distress has been observed by researchers; however, no significant relationship existed between perceived discrimination and perceived life quality, which included health satisfaction (Forman, 2003). Thus, although perceived discrimination seems to be a constant in the lives of Black people, there are other factors at play that can buffer it.

## AN OUNCE OF PREVENTION

Community-based health programs hold the most promise when it comes to effecting change. Such interventions that would consider cultural components are sorely needed in communities of African descent. Those programs that coalesce with the community stand a good chance of fitting the bill of providing services in a culturally competent manner. Such was the aim in community-based participatory research, one of the ways to build prevention programming. Corbie-Smith et al. (2011) described the development of Project GRACE (Growing, Reaching, Advocating for Change and Empowerment) using this method. They built their partnership in four stages: "initial mobilization" (involving the community from the beginning at grant proposal), "establishing organizational structure" (setting up committees and guidelines for operating), "capacity building for action" (including process evaluation), and "planning for action." The largest share of Project GRACE consisted of community members, at 25%.

One innovative prevention program took place in the community around a single setting: hair salons. The development of the BEAUTY program (Bringing Education and Understanding to You) was dependent on the advisory board which consisted of community members and reached out to beauticians who provided input about health topics they discussed with their patrons. Linnan and Ferguson (2007) recognized the "potential to reinforce health messages" of the salons. They found that cancer prevention efforts could be driven by fruit/vegetable intake and conversations about it. As is the case with many community-based efforts, participants were concerned about sustainability.

Health equity can be achieved if prevention programs are culturally grounded, according to Harvey and Afful (2011), and should consist of racial identity, as it was correlated with health promoting behaviors in their study. The research participants were mostly middle-income African American women whose average age was 23; they were asked to rate health promoting or health compromising behaviors as typically Black or typically white, in addition to whether they engaged in those behaviors or not. Those who embraced a nationalist identity were more likely to engage in health promoting behaviors that they deemed as typically Black.

The case for culturally based prevention programs for African-descended populations has been supported consistently by the research. For instance, Beatty et al. (2004) and Gillum (2008) proposed as much and more. Beatty et al. (2004) focus on HIV prevention programming and their ideas would be easily promoted in other prevention programming as well. They include the use of theories to guide research specifically reflective of Black people with a recognition of their inherent variety. The researchers did not limit their focus to individual behavior like so many prevention programs, but also suggested the targeting of environmental and structural factors for change as well. Etowa and Hyman (2021) proposed for African-descended populations in Canada that evidence-based interventions should tackle social determinants of health and community-based programming should be aimed at promoting optimal health.

A host of prevention programming with African-descended people includes a focus on HIV prevention. Many of those programs have enlisted churches to build an infrastructure designed to reach out to its community members. Since religiosity/spirituality are identified as a key cultural strength, its protective aspects, cloaked under the auspices of the Black church, are in a good position to play a huge role in HIV prevention. My church has been a leader in this effort in the community for years by providing HIV testing monthly to congregants and participating in the AIDS Walk. Wooster et al. (2011) surveyed faith communities in the southside of Chicago, Harlem, Hinds County in Mississippi, and Maricopa County in Arizona. Not only did many participants across all sites note a change in attitudes among their community members about HIV prevention, but also when pastors took the lead in providing HIV testing, it simultaneously decreased its perceived stigma among members of their respective congregations. On the other hand, fundamentalist doctrine/conservatism (a literal reading of the Bible) of a faith leader was a barrier toward HIV prevention.

Another HIV prevention program, TEACH (Training and Empowering African American Churches on HIV/AIDS), yielded rich data when Piper et al. (2020) conducted a qualitative study with women churchgoers whose average age was 47. Six themes emerged which included controlling the sexual health narrative, churches' expectations for men's and women's sexuality, gender role expectations of parents, expectations for children's sexuality, enacting sexual scripts, and sexual agency/submission. Piper et al. (2020) noted that their findings revealed that the participants reported feeling more emboldened as they aged, challenging church norms so that they would do better.

There are many HIV prevention programs that target Black populations, and a few target LGBT+ individuals. Social support is key for intervention programs to work, especially for the communal orientation among African-descended populations. The importance of social support was noted in an intervention with Black men who had sex with men (MSM); some of them were Black Latino, which is rarely parsed out in the literature. Most of the men had finished high school and their ages ranged from 18 to 29. Eke et al. (2019) found that social support from their Black friends was negatively correlated with having unprotected sex and positively correlated with knowledge about their status. Another HIV prevention program in South Africa designed for girls and women, whose ages ranged from 15 to 2424, also revealed the importance of social support. The participants noted in this qualitative study that the influences of partners and caregivers played a role in access to contraception. Jonas et al. (2020) suggested that not including the role of social support could compromise the effectiveness of such programs.

In much of the HIV prevention research, MSM are targeted, but a growing number of researchers are addressing MSM and men who have sex with women (MSW) but do not identify as gay or bisexual (Arnold et al., 2019; Lauby et al., 2018). The Bruthas Project was developed with community input and meant to address this population. In their intervention program, the average age of the participants was 45 and almost three- quarters of them were not employed. They were more likely to use condoms with men, women, and transwomen due to program participation compared to the men in the control group (Arnold et al., 2019). The inclusion of the community in the design of this program is in line with best practices for interventions designed with people of African descent in mind.

However, just because the community is involved does not translate to the program automatically considering cultural considerations. In one program that did, the Men in Life Environments (also an HIV intervention program), racial identity, assessed as racial pride, was found to be related to use of condoms with men and women through condom use self-efficacy among men who did not have HIV. Almost a third of the sample was HIV positive and the average age of the participants was 40. The same pattern of associations was not found among the HIV- positive men, although racial pride was positively correlated with condom use self-efficacy (Li et al., 2018). Another program for African American girls and women, ranging in age from 15 to 62 was the WISH (Women's Initiative for Sexual Health) program which targeted the prevention of HIV. Robinson et al. (2005) assessed acculturation as part of the program and found that it did not predict condom use or high-risk sexual behavior while attitudes toward condoms predicted consistent condom use.

Prevention of intimate partner violence is paramount for optimal functioning among African-descended romantic partners. Gillum (2008) offered that IPV prevention programming should focus on both men and women with an awareness of getting away from stereotypes and (I would say) to decrease the internalized racism that may contribute to abusive behavior in the first place. In her research, she interviewed not just staff members involved in an intervention program but also survivors who had benefited from their services. The average age of the survivors was 40 and the founder of the program was African American. The survivors reported being in an environment which made them feel safe; they used spirituality as a coping mechanism.

Gillum (2008) suggested that IPV interventions when targeting Black people should be culturally specific to be effective. How would that prevention program look? A review of the research by her suggests, among others, that (1) involving the community is key because they know best what they need; (2) staff should look like the community the intervention is aiming to serve; and (3) language, values, and attitudes, among others, of the community must be included in the design of the overall program.

There are quite a few prevention programs that target obesity among African-descended people by endorsing healthy diets, promoting exercise, and varied activities. The SHAPE Program was designed for Black women whose average age was 36. They received accelerometers while exercise and nutrition information were provided. Greaney et al. (2017) reported that the program did not impact exercise, but the participants did lose weight, possibly due to changes in diet.

Obesity is not just a problem in the Western world, but also around the world, as Western diets are exported to other countries through genetically modified foods and sugary carbonated drinks. Renzaho et al. (2015) recognized this in the development of their prevention program in conjunction with the community meant to be helped. The Healthy Migrant Families Initiative: Challenges and Choices, designed for African migrant communities in Australia, consisted of two modules—"Healthy Families in a New Culture" and "Healthy Lifestyles in a New Culture"—involving several sessions.

Peer education is key in many community outreach programs as well. It serves to move us toward better health and intervention measures. Black women volunteered to be peer educators in a study by Hempstead et al. (2018). They were trained to be community empowerment partners, tasked with outreach to African American women. Their focus was breast cancer education and workshops. Cierra Sisters, a breast cancer support organization by and for Black women, was involved from the start. Most of the community empowerment partners and workshop participants were over 40 years of age. Community members reported more knowledge than they did at the beginning of the workshops. Hempstead et al. (2018) saw "using peer educators . . . [as] culturally relevant" (p. 839). In another study, Tobin et al. (2018) reported on a peer mentoring program for Black men having sex with men. The participants, whose average age was 26, were asked about their willingness to participate in being a peer mentor and interviewed about their experiences as such within their social circles. Some of the peer mentors were HIV-negative but their experiences did not differ significantly from HIV-positive peer mentors.

Prevention programming is key to alleviating health challenges among African-descended people. Context plays a large role in health promotion and should be considered when designing such programming. This is where health psychology in cultural context would be impactful. During the COVID-19 pandemic, churches and HBCUs have provided invaluable services to the surrounding Black community by providing testing and vaccinations. Interventions and prevention work hand in hand for promoting health. In the next chapter, we will see how this works for African-descended youth.

# Chapter 5

# Cherishing the Children

Much of the literature on children of African descent operates from a deficit model. In other words, the focus is usually on risk factors and the negative behaviors in which the youth may engage. Examining behavior using a strengths model by concentrating on protective factors will be explored in this chapter, in keeping with the theme of the book. The impact of families, mass media, schools, and community will all be considered.

I want to focus your attention not only on the protective aspects of racial identity against negative life outcomes, but also on its properties against racial discrimination as well. In a lot of ways, cultural identity feeds into the resilience that could be honed by young people, beginning in childhood. Researchers have found that the belongingness and affirmation parts of cultural identity may be the specific protective parts likely to heighten awareness of racism (Banks et al., 2021; Stock et al., 2011).

Resilience is a key piece of how health promotion would work for children of African descent. A recent study speaks to this and could be instructive in this COVID-19 age. A longitudinal study by Brody et al. (2020) found that planned self-control predicted fewer depressive symptoms. While years in poverty did not predict depression, childhood adversity did predict it. This seems to indicate that the experience of poverty is not enough to suggest that a person will be depressed; however, childhood adversity does. This is akin to how researchers focus on family structure when the functioning of a family plays a bigger role in impacting one's childhood. Extended families are more likely to exist among African-descended populations. Our conception of family should go beyond parents to embrace the term *caregivers* for children being raised by other relatives.

The relationship between resilience and ethnic identity was noted in a study among adolescents living in Tanzania. They were given the developmental assets profile (DAP) translated into Swahili (Drescher et al., 2018). They also took the MEIM (multigroup ethnic identity measure), among a number of other measures. This ethnic identity measure correlated positively with the DAP and predicted general self-efficacy.

Some of us had assumptions about how children were doing anecdotally during the COVID-19 pandemic, but the question of how they were really doing was answered in a qualitative study by Parker et al. (2021). They asked seven boys and five girls, ranging in age from 12 to 17, about their challenges and how they were coping during the pandemic. Some of the key issues the participants noted were the challenge of online work and having more work assigned by their teachers. Another study even found that teachers gave more work due to the perception of making up for lack of face-to-face interaction. Parker et al. (2021) also found that the youth felt closer to their families, having had time to interact with them. They did note missing their friends and many of them drew on their religiosity/spirituality. Social support came from school counselors, for some of the children who mentioned it.

The common theme of cultural identity as healthy for one's mental health was seen in a study by Ahn et al. (2021). The mostly African American and African Caribbean adolescents who participated in their study had an average age of 15; they were middle class and almost 60% of them were girls. The researchers reported negative correlations between internalizing behaviors (anxiety/depressed and withdrawn/depressed) and ethnic identity (affirmation). Mandara et al. (2009) reported negative correlations existed between racial identity and depression among boys and girls in seventh grade. For eighth grade boys, racial identity was negatively correlated with anxiety. The researchers also reported that racial identity in seventh grade was negatively related with depression in eighth grade among adolescent boys; furthermore, the higher their racial identity, the lower their depression.

We have known for years that some aspects of cultural identity are related to fewer positive attitudes toward risky behavior. For example, Black girls whose average age was 11 were asked about their religiosity, cultural identity, and attitudes toward sex, among other variables in a study by Belgrave et al. (2000). Ethnic identity negatively predicted risky sexual and pregnancy attitudes. High religiosity was not related to risky attitudes and suggests that we have to go beyond religiosity to cultural identity to buffer these attitudes. Locke and Newcomb (2008) categorized cultural pride and healthy relational attachment as part of the mesosystem for adolescent girls. The average age of participants in their sample was around 17 and most had been pregnant at some point. More cultural pride translated to less drug use.

In some cases, ethnic identity has been predictive of drug use and sexual risk taking. Such a relationship was found in a study by Opara et al. (2020) among Black girls in high school. Ethnic identity was not only negatively related to past 30 days drug use but also predicted it. Ethnic identity was negative correlated with sexual risk-taking behavior as well; however, past

30 days drug use mediated the relationship between these two variables. The researchers also found that ethnic identity was positively correlated to psychological empowerment and social support.

## CREATIVE PARENTING

How we cherish our children sets the stage for future optimal mental and physical health. I was in a clinic with my daughter one day and another mom was there with her son. He looked about 3 or 4 and was very active. (As an aside, I often tell parents not to call their children "bad" because it calls attention to their perceived essence, rather than to their behavior.) The mother kept saying to him "come here, little (n-word)" and was abrasive to him. My daughter looked at me wide-eyed. Rather than tell her how she should talk to her son, I commented "your son is adorable" and we made small talk. By the time we went into the doctor's office a few minutes later, we noticed she was handling her son more kindly and had stopped calling him names.

Parental or caregiver support is key to optimal health outcomes. For example, Vazsony, et al. (2006) studied youth of African descent ranging in age from 10 to 19, and they found that the warmth and discipline of the parents with their children explained whether the youth would engage in health-compromising behaviors. The researchers believed that the resilience of the youth was enhanced due to these parenting processes. Mother and father support were negatively related to alcohol use in a study by Caldwell et al. (2004). However, parental support and racial identity operated together to predict alcohol use among Black adolescents whose average age was 17; a bit over half of them were girls. The families were blue collar on average. Father support and private regard were key to these predictions. Centrality moderated the relationship between alcohol use and private regard. Landor et al. (2019) found that dark skinned women who had high parental support maintained their self-esteem. Their longitudinal study followed young African American women since fifth grade who were asked about racial identity and negative sexual health outcomes, among other variables. Racial identity's positive correlation with self-esteem and sexual behavior speaks once again to its impact on health outcomes.

On the other hand, non-supportive parenting can result in negative health outcomes. This issue was studied by Beach et al. (2014) who noted its relationship to telomere length among African American adolescents followed over a five-year period beginning on average around the age of 17. The researchers found not only was non-supportive parenting related to telomere length, but also that increased substance use mediated the relationship at age 22. Shortened telomere length is related to a host of disease processes.

When we talk about health promotion and African-descended people, we sometimes forget to include those with disabilities. It takes a special kind of parenting to raise children with disabilities and it often reflects a community of care ethos. Coping and family functioning were positively correlated in a study by Algood and Davis (2019) of experiences of families of children with disabilities. Of the participants, 38% reported severe disability; most of the children had speech or language impairments with orthopedic impairments coming in second. Resilience was key to explaining why the family thrived despite such challenges. The average age of the children was 10 years; those with traumatic brain injuries resulted in heavier loads embraced by caregivers.

Autism is rapidly growing as a disability that some children experience. However, there is not a lot of research examining Black parents' perceptions of it in their children. Hannon et al. (2018) was one of the few who did so, conducting qualitative research with six African American fathers of children with autism. The children (five boys and one girl) ranged in age from 5 to 22, and the fathers were married with college degrees. Patience was a prominent theme in the fathers' interview responses. Hannon et al. (2018) also suggested that racial socialization needs to be considered when working with Black fathers as well as the ways the fathers in this study experienced a form of post-traumatic growth.

## RACIAL DISCRIMINATION

The relationship between racial discrimination and health outcomes has been studied among African-descended children. For instance, Carter et al. (2019) assessed the consequences of childhood discrimination on later life outcomes. They found that children's experience of racial discrimination was correlated with depression in their 20s. Although discrimination did not have a direct relationship with accelerated aging, it was related to accelerated aging indirectly through depression. The study's findings suggest that attributing health outcomes to racial discrimination paints a complicated picture.

There is a need to include racial discrimination as a community or societal impact not only on children's behavior, but also its effects on their genes. Chae et al. (2020) examined the relationship between racial discrimination and telomere shortening. Telomere shortening is linked to the aging process, which may be premature for some populations, depending on their experiences (in addition to disease processes, as previously mentioned). The researchers found that telomere length at age 15 was negatively correlated with smoking behavior. Smoking was associated with shortened telomeres. Telomere length at age 15 was positively correlated with telomere length at age 25. They also found that racial discrimination at age 15 was positively correlated to racial discrimination at age 25 (Chae et al., 2020).

Sometimes the community in which a child lives does not make a difference in their feelings about their racial identity. An example would be Hurd et al. (2013) who reported a negative relationship between racial identity and depression, regardless of whether the participants' neighborhood was Black majority or Black minority, over a five-year period, beginning, on average, around the age of 17. In other words, the higher one's private regard about their racial identity, the less likely they were to experience depression.

Racial discrimination contributes to health problems, but the question of which health problems is still emerging. What is becoming clear is that there is a difference in impact on health over time between consistently high racial discrimination and initially low but increasing experiences of racism. Brody et al. (2018) found in their longitudinal study of African American adolescents that racial discrimination (ages 16–18) impacted insulin resistance (ages 25–27) and body mass index (BMI) (ages 19–21). (As an aside, insulin resistance can lead to diabetes.) For BMI, participants reporting high racial discrimination were affected at twice the level of those reporting low but increasing racial discrimination. Those experiencing consistently high racist events were also more likely to have their insulin resistance impacted, compared to low but increasing racial discrimination. Additionally, Brody et al. (2018) found that BMI mediated the relationship between high racial discrimination in adolescence and insulin resistance; insulin resistance was influenced by a high number of racist events through BMI. Finally, they reported a positive correlation between substance use and both racial discrimination and depression.

This finding makes the case for parents who wish to give their children a healthy start. Parents and caregivers, armed with the knowledge that exposing their children to high racial discrimination may affect their BMI or insulin resistance, might make different choices for them, setting the stage for their future optimal health. One study by Gibbons et al. (2021) examined the relationship between perceived racial discrimination, optimism, and healthy behaviors, assessing diet (fruit/vegetable intake) and exercise. The researchers found that optimism moderated the relationship between perceived racial discrimination and healthy behaviors for girls but not for boys.

Many caregivers are realizing that a choice may exist between their child's health and mostly white environments, often the source of consistently high racial discrimination. Protecting the child's health, even before the adolescent years, is crucial; thus, a diverse or mostly Black environment may be warranted as one way to ensure low racial discrimination that may increase over time. Perhaps the ability to develop a sense of self, enhanced by not having to think about racial discrimination too much, also sets the stage for the body to mature in a more ideal manner. The finding about the role of optimism should be considered as well.

In one longitudinal study assessing perceived discrimination, the focus was on how African American adolescents (almost half were boys) felt about the vibes from teachers. Fuller-Rowell et al. (2012) noted a negative correlation between public regard and perceived discrimination from one point in time to the other. Perceived discrimination at one point was associated with both substance use and perceived discrimination at a later point in time. When adolescents with high public regard experienced perceived discrimination at a high level at time one, their substance use was higher compared to those with low public regard.

Previously mentioned studies have noted the importance of racial socialization in a child's life so that the child is able to buffer the effects of racial discrimination. Deliberately raising children so that they are racially socialized also counters the appropriation of racism. Stevenson et al. (2002) reported cultural identity as protective in allowing a young person to detect discrimination and negotiate volatile situations, and proactive when it includes "cultural pride reinforcement" and "cultural legacy appreciation." They found that cultural identity was associated with fewer fights and fewer instances of initiating fights among Black boys and girls whose average age was 14.

## FAMILY MATTERS

Family has been found to be protective against depression. Fitzpatrick et al. (2005) found that social capital (family, school, and religious variables) among 10–18-year-old youth was a buffer against depression for girls and older adolescents. In another study by Street et al. (2009) both ethnic identity and family functioning (specifically cohesion) predicted depression in adolescents, meaning that higher ethnic identity predicted lower depression. The average age of the participants was 12 and included parents who were middle income.

The relationship between racial/ethnic/cultural identity and depression has been fairly consistent. Ethnic identity was negatively related to depression, aggressive beliefs, and aggressive behavior among mostly Black adolescents whose ages ranged from 10 to 15 in a study by McMahon and Watts (2002); 60% of them were girls. The researchers also reported that high ethnic identity predicted both fewer aggressive beliefs and behavior; yet global self-worth predicted aggressive beliefs. This is similar to the previous findings that high self-esteem is related to high aggressive tendencies. The task for us is to raise our children so that their self-esteem is moderate; low is bad and high may be worse.

## GOOD EATING

Years ago, I worked with junior high school students in Fifth Ward, Houston, Texas who were participating in a family and community violence prevention program. During breaks, the children would go to the local convenience store and come back with candies, chips, and soda. We discussed the idea of our bringing snacks to the program that were healthy for them, compared to what they were consuming. We recognized the importance of nutrition in developing healthy behaviors from an early age.

Obesity among African-descended children has been challenging. Alexander et al. (2015) explored how caregivers perceived childhood obesity. Most of the caregivers had completed some college and were employed, between the ages of 25 and 35, and included a small percentage of men. Half of the families had between three and five children. Their thoughts about obesity would be classified as environmental, as the participants reported that schools and doctors played a part in preventing obesity. A little over half were concerned about their children's weight and believed education about low-fat meals and eating healthy was warranted.

Some have suggested that part of the reason that Black girls experience obesity is that they are concerned about "sweating" out their hair. Woolford et al. (2016) explored this notion and reported a positive association between ethnic identity and physical activity among African-descended adolescent girls. They were also more likely to exercise if they had hair extensions.

I often tell students that the way they eat and exercise now sets the stage for how they will age. Cardiovascular risk can be predicted by BMI, blood pressure, and A1c levels as early as 29 years of age (Lei et al., 2018). The researchers did just that in their study examining its relationship to childhood trauma, diet, and exercise, among other variables. Childhood trauma and cardiovascular risk were positively correlated. Puberty mediated this relationship such that BMI and blood pressure were affected among children followed longitudinally since an average age of 10 years. No gender differences existed, and one could ask whether there is a version of the Childhood

Trauma Questionnaire that includes any questions related to discrimination, as those experiences may be traumatic as well to Black children.

## MORE THAN "JUST SAY NO"

The relationship between cultural identity and substance use has garnered mixed findings. In some studies, cultural identity was positively correlated with substance use. Other researchers have reported negative correlations between these two variables. For example, negative correlations were found between cultural identity and substance use, depression, anxiety, and racial discrimination in a study of African American adolescents, almost 60% of whom were girls and mostly eighth graders (Zapolski et al., 2018). Cultural identity was conceptualized as collective self-esteem. Cultural identity predicted fewer depressive and anxiety symptoms, while feeling positively about one's ethnic group predicted lower substance use. In another study by Arsenault et al. (2018) not only was ethnic identity related to lower marijuana use but school engagement mediated the relationship between the two variables among African American high school students where no gender differences were noted.

Racial socialization appears to play a role in resistance to substance use. In one study where most of the mothers had some college education, participants (whose average age was around 16) reported on their experiences with racial socialization, ethnic identity, and attitudes toward substance use, among other variables (Wallace & Fisher, 2007). Awareness of racial discrimination, ethnic identity, peer attitudes, and parental attitudes all predicted adolescents' disapproval of substance use.

## RELIGIOUS CAVEATS

There are protective aspects of religiosity and spirituality that have been found among African-descended youth populations. For instance, among a sample of mostly Black seventh and eighth grade adolescents, religion was inversely correlated with aggressive behavior. Specifically, the importance of religion and church attendance reduced the likelihood of involvement in aggression (Clubb et al., 2001). In another study, psychological well-being was examined among African American girls, whose average age was 15, by Butler-Barnes et al. (2018). They asked the girls about their religiosity and the degree to which they internalized racial stigma. The researchers reported a positive correlation between racial de-stigmatization (in other words, their rejection of racial stigma) and both their relationship with God and their psychological well-being. They found religiosity was positively related to psychological well-being and protected against racial stigma. African American and African Caribbean youth between the ages of 13 to 17 were asked about their racial identity, religiosity, and sexual initiation. High religiosity predicted lower instances of sexual initiation; their private regard scores were also elevated in this study, designed to explore interactions between racial identity and religiosity (Taggart et al., 2019).

For years, Black girls have been told to be good girls by our religious institutions. Many of them assume that going to a Black church is part of the culture, but if the church is not actively teaching culture, then there continues to be no difference between adolescent behavior in the church and in the "world." Some of these churches have imagery of white people as God and saints in their images. This has the unintended consequence of feeding into internalized racism.

In one study, ethnic identity commitment and exploration were found to be positively correlated to adolescent religious beliefs by Halgunseth et al. (2016). The average age of the participants was about 16, and about half were girls. While mothers' and fathers' beliefs and practices were positively correlated, adolescents' beliefs and practices were also positively associated with both parents. This speaks to the importance of cultural transmission in the lives of children, as well as the need for ensuring that religiosity and cultural identity are concordant.

The relationship between religiosity and alcohol use is complicated. For instance, religiosity was not related to any alcohol risk behaviors in a study by Nasim et al. (2007); however, Afrocentrism was related to these behaviors among Black adolescents (about half were boys) whose average age was around 16. The researchers reported negative correlations between Afrocentrism and both peer risk behaviors and lifetime alcohol use. Alcohol initiation was positively related to Afrocentrism. It may be due to family endorsement and pouring liquor for the "brothers who ain't here" (a nod to the movie *Cooley High*), a spiritual behavior. Religiosity and peer risk behavior worked together to predict alcohol initiation and Afrocentrism negatively predicted lifetime alcohol use. As an aside, a little over half of the participants never drank alcohol.

## SEXUAL HEALTH

Conflicting information given to boys and girls is the hallmark of varying sexual health outcomes. While boys are often told to sow their wild oats, girls are not encouraged to do the same. Additionally, they are given messages regarding contraception and the onus is often on the girl as she is the responsible one and could end up pregnant. These differences in messaging account for differences in attitudes. Freeman et al. (1980) found as much in an earlier study comparing attitudes of boys and girls. The researchers also wanted to see if the differences would be dependent on where the information emanated. There were over 700 participants (mostly 10th and 11th graders) from three high schools and a teen clinic. However, they did not mention needing the parents' permission to participate.

Freeman et al. (1980) found that most of the youth did not know when girls were more likely to be pregnant. There were no differences in overall knowledge between girls at the school and those from the clinic. While the girls' knowledge improved between 10th and 12th grade, boys' knowledge leveled off and decreased slightly between those two grades. Boys' knowledge level was explained by their dependence on girls' knowledge, and the researchers recommended sex education for younger students, before high school.

HIV research has been prominent over many decades; among adolescents, there are few exceptions. In a qualitative study, African American adolescents between the ages of 13 and 17 reported that "internalizing racial situations could contribute to an adolescent's HIV risk" (Sidibe et al., 2018, p. 18). This is similar to findings in other research outlining the relationship between appropriated racial oppression and risky sexual behavior. There is a danger to the racialized idea of Black girls and boys as inherently highly sexualized. Believing this stereotype about themselves, without racial socialization to offset this, may explain risky sexual behavior. The girls in this study also talked about not being able to see their peers as support due to how a girl might be perceived by others. Consequently, Sidibe et al. (2018) suggested that HIV-prevention programs for youth should include anti-bullying components.

## PREVENTION PROGRESS

Interventions for African-descended populations in general (and children in particular) are most effective if they are culturally grounded. Racial socialization can be impacted in some of these programs, which can result in positive health outcomes in the long run. Coard et al. (2004) asked parents about their child-rearing practices. Most of the parents of 5- to 6-year-old children were mothers whose average age was 34. The researchers identified four core themes in their study: racism preparation, racial pride, racial equality, and racial achievement. Parents reported that they role played and modeled behavior they wanted their children to internalize.

We talked throughout this book about the importance of involving the Black community in health promotion. An HIV prevention program targeting mostly Black 10th- and 11th-grade youth resulted in positive attitudes toward condoms as well as increased condom self-efficacy in the DHAB A (decreasing HIV/AIDS boldly) and BART (becoming a responsible teen) conditions reported by Holliday et al. (2020). Over two-thirds of the participants were girls in this community- based participatory research. DHAB A is akin to what other researchers and I did with students in the violence prevention program. Because this was before the advent of social media, we asked the junior high youth to write and act in a play based on what they had learned in the program.

My dissertation examined substance abuse prevention programming for African American children in sixth grade. The program involved cultural components such as racial identity and Afrocentric values orientation. Chipungu et al. (2000) examined substance abuse prevention programming and found that many programs aimed at Black children were particularly likely to include considerations of culture as well. They found that the programs were playing a role in racially socializing the children and targeting alcohol, tobacco, and other drug use simultaneously. Most of the programs at that time served children under the age of 12, 20% of whom were being reared by extended family members. The finding that Black students in the substance abuse prevention programs with an Afrocentric orientation liked their programs better than the Black students in one-size-fits-all substance abuse prevention programs was particularly telling.

Many programs targeting young people of African descent historically were not culturally based. I would posit, based on earlier discussions in this book, that this may occur because Black people are often seen as not having a culture. One of the few exceptions was that reported by Tolmach (1985); findings from a program designed to help Black youth between the ages of 12 and 22 were described. The day treatment program, City Lights, endorsed an approach that did not encourage medication for 30 youth. Counseling was available for the student who was typically 16. The cultural component was rooted in the arts; aiming to form a choir, the musician met with the youth weekly. Furthermore, they were connected to the Black community through the churches. An early version of telehealth with the use of teletherapy was used as part of the individual therapy component. Over a 3-year period, most of the youth experienced positive outcomes.

The City Lights program recognized the importance of culture by connecting its clients to the community; reporting involving the community in initial designs would have been promising as well. As an aside, the mental health profession may be more open to allowing this, as the medical profession sees three races in their training and treats them accordingly (Democracy Now, 2020). Treating the race, rather than the culture, gets health professionals in trouble consistently and tends to make them less effective in their treatments (TED, 2016).

It would be difficult to write a book about health psychology for African-descended populations without including issues of violence, particularly among boys. Bryant (2011) stated, "It could well be that the acceptance of violence against African Americans for much of this country's [United States] history creates a context in which impoverished African American youth are more willing to engage in acts of violence against each other" (p. 694), in his critique of mainstream analyses of violence in the Black community in both history and context. Bryant (2011) found that internalized racism predicted proclivity toward violence, while racial identity protected against it. He also suggested that if a policy is to help Black boys, we might consider screening them for internalized racism as generic measures failed to adequately explain the variance in violence propensity. This study is Amos Wilson's theoretical orientation about violence exemplified.

Violence prevention is key to optimal health among African-descended people; programs related to this should begin in early adolescent years. The relationship between cultural identity and violence prevention has been noted in a few studies. One study was designed for African American boys ranging in age from 8 to 14. Okwumabua et al. (1999) measured how they felt about their racial identity, self-esteem, and decision-making processes after participating in the program, which included conflict resolution. Both their racial identity and conflict resolution skills increased due to the program's effect. One of the activities the boys participated in included visiting sites connected to their heritage.

Not too many prevention programs tackle suicide risk. An innovative one that considered culture was the A-CWS (adapted-coping with stress) program. Robinson et al. (2016) developed the program for African American adolescents who were in high school. Suicide risk was reduced by 86%, a remarkable number. They noted the decreasing suicide risk by targeting stressors was a winning formula.

A few interventions have promoted healthy eating. One example is the B'more Healthy Communities for Kids intervention, meant to improve food access for children. The average age of the children in the study by Gittelsohn et al. (2017) was 11; the program went beyond targeting how participants and their caregivers ate to what local markets had to offer. Over two- thirds of them participated in SNAP (Supplemental Assistance Nutrition Program). The researchers found that the intervention spurred children to purchase promoted healthy snacks, compared to their caregivers; those not participating in the program also increased their access.

The relationship between cultural identity and health behaviors is most often studied in young people. However, cultural values are most apparent among the elderly. In the next chapter, we will see how cultural values and health behaviors appear for older Black populations.

# Chapter 6

# Empowering the Elderly

The concept of resilience, a major theme of this book, seems to be key to the health of Black people over the age of 50. I want to focus on ways we can empower the elderly so that they maintain agency over their lives. Interventions for the elderly will also be discussed in this chapter.

COVID-19 has had a devastating effect on elderly African-descended populations. McDuffie (2021) noted that isolation and bereavement continued to impact their mental health and contributed to their many stressors. Also, the potential cultural buffers of kinship and spirituality are being challenged. Those cultural factors have been thwarted by the pandemic, leaving older Black people with fewer tools for addressing the stressors. It is a good idea to check on the elderly consistently and introduce them to new ways to be connected, such as technology like FaceTime or Zoom.

One way to reach out to the African-descended elderly populations includes having a mobile unit, described by Alcaraz et al. (2011). The Neighborhood Voice provided outreach regarding breast cancer by assessing, intervening, and following up with African American women in targeted communities. Although the average age of their participants was 58, not only would it provide accessibility to all Black people, but it would also enable them to feel more comfortable participating in research that could best serve their interests. The researchers found that most of the women were satisfied with their experiences; their comfort and convenience predicted this (Alcaraz et al., 2011).

There is a wide range of mental and physical health outcomes for older Black people. One example is a grandmother who has continued working because she finds value in her job. In another instance, a great-grandfather still exercises regularly and runs marathons on his birthday. Even in challenging stories, a great-great-grandmother evicted from her home she shared with a daughter, due to a confidentiality breach by the state's adult protective agency, is now living in comfort surrounded by those who love her.

Screening for diseases such as colon cancer has been explored among older Black people. Rather than stopping at asking why Black people do not get colonoscopies, Klasko-Foster et al. (2019) asked under what conditions do Black people participate in colon cancer screening? Environmental factors were considered in their research. The average age of the participants hovered around 65, and they were mostly women. Trust in and satisfaction with the doctor were critical to getting a colonoscopy. The participants in this study consisted of African Americans and African Caribbeans. In other research, self-efficacy and positive attitude toward getting a colonoscopy were positively correlated to colonoscopy screening in a study by Kiviniemi et al. (2018). The average age of the African Americans in their study was a little over 66 years of age.

Some intervention programs make a concerted effort to reach out to community locales other than churches. For instance, a patient-navigated intervention resulted in twice as many older Black men who decided to be screened for colorectal cancer, compared to those assessed only for blood pressure. Cole et al. (2017) reported on the effects of the MISTER B intervention (Multi-Intervention Study to Improve CRC Screening and to Enhance Risk Reduction in Black Men). The men, whose average age hovered around 57, were recruited from barbershops. Over 20% had no insurance, and 40% had not seen a doctor in the past year. Although many of them had high blood pressure, they also reported having high physical activity levels.

Despite neighborhood locales, Black people do engage in physical activity. An example for negotiating taking walks was studied by Child et al. (2019). They noted that most of the participants in their qualitative study exercised and enjoyed connecting with others in the neighborhood. The mostly Black women had an average age of 61. They did mention the lack of sidewalks as a safety issue but recognized walking as a good way to stay healthy. I find this to be the case in many older residential neighborhoods.

One of the few studies to examine the relationship between racial identity and perceptions about cancer was offered by Lucas et al. (2018). Over half of their sample were between 49 and 55. Most of the participants made over $25,000 USD per year and had completed some college. Racial identity (centrality) was positively related to intention to undergo colorectal cancer screening. Those low in racial identity exposed to the culturally targeted program were more receptive to the gain- framed messages. On the other hand, those who were high in racial identity were more receptive to the loss- framed messages. The gain-framed message was "Timeliness can be beneficial," while the loss-framed message was "Delay can be costly."

## THE SUGAR

Diabetes is one of many debilitating diseases affecting Black populations. It is often linked to nutrition and exercise. While some researchers place priority on changing food preparation practices and physical activity, it would be a better idea to encourage alternatives that are palatable and culturally grounded, as stated in a previous chapter.

When people have been cooking and eating in a certain manner all of their lives, it is difficult to make changes. One program that attempted to encourage its participants toward change was the HEAL-D intervention. Moore et al. (2019) conducted research among Africans and African Caribbean people living in London whose average age was 62; 46% of them were retired and almost a quarter of them had tertiary education. In their focus groups, they discussed diet and exercise to manage diabetes. The participants interpreted being told by health care practitioners to reduce the amount of carbs as "don't eat your traditional foods." But they also reported that social support was important in mitigating the effects of diabetes. They noted they were being told to exercise but not being given clarity on how this should look. Participants in the Moore et al. (2019) study believed they moved around enough and may not have needed the gym because "going to the gym is not in my culture" (p. 1155). Many of them walked or danced; exercise seems to be best supported by collective movement, as mentioned in a previous study.

In another study examining the impact of diabetes, the relationship between resilience and A1c levels among Black women was explored by DeNisco (2011). In her study, the average age of the participants was 55 and included African Americans, African Caribbeans, and Africans. Almost 30% were working poor, over one- third had disabilities, and a quarter of them had diabetes for at least three years. The researcher reported a negative correlation between resilience and HbA1c levels. In other words, A1c levels were likely to fluctuate due to resilience levels.

Empowering Black people toward health equity would increase their resilience. Involving the community in designing health promotion interventions is critical to giving a voice to individuals most affected by disease processes. Many programs geared toward the elderly involve cultural components that are most often reflective of religiosity or spirituality. Oftentimes, they are community based with the assumption that they will be cultural.

## THE COLLECTIVE

Social support from family and friends is often mentioned as crucial for those surviving many diseases, including cancer. Mobilizing a collective to be in one's corner when one is facing a deadly illness impacts the mental health of not just the one with the disease, but also members of one's communal group.

Participants ranging in age from 50 to above 80 were asked about their beliefs about colon cancer and affiliated screenings. The largest percentage of them were middle income, and about half were men (Brittain & Murphy, 2015). Collectivism as a cultural value was positively correlated with colorectal cancer beliefs as well as religiosity, which was also positively correlated with colonoscopy as a screening preference. It would have been interesting to run analyses examining the relationship between the cultural variables and other health variables they assessed such as high blood pressure, diabetes, and high cholesterol. The researchers found that religiosity and having a primary care provider predicted colonoscopy. The fecal occult blood test (FOBT) was predicted by collectivism, present time orientation, and informed decision about colorectal cancer screenings.

Spirituality and social support seem to work together in research about older African-descended people. For example, the experiences of Black men with prostate cancer in Canada were explored by Gray et al. (2005) who interviewed them. In this case study, the men discussed spirituality and social support in coping. They also believed that they were more than their cancers; they wanted to talk about other issues besides the prostate cancer diagnosis. One of the participants noted the lack of health communication and advocated for himself, and another suggested that doctors might consider talking to significant others about negotiating side effects.

In another study, older rural Black men who were prostate cancer survivors were asked about how their faith informed their physical and psychological health in a study by Adams and Johnson (2021). The men ranged in age from 65 to 78, and most had college degrees. Spirituality was a common theme in their answers, regardless of religious affiliation (or non-affiliation), and social support also played a key role in their recovery. The researchers noted that their participants did not feed into the strong silent stereotype of men who would handle their health by themselves.

## I SAY A LITTLE PRAYER

The importance of religiosity and spirituality for elderly Black people cannot be dismissed. For instance, positions in the church as deacons, ushers, choir members, or church mothers become a core part of their identity as they age. This differs for those who may embrace other religions.

Some decide to go into the ministry as they get older. In one study which included African American ministers whose average age was 51, Stansbury et al. (2018) interviewed them about the way they provided counseling to their older congregants. The participants described their duties as "shepherding the flock," which involved "pastoral awareness, pastoral screening, pastoral counseling, internal ministries, and follow up with elders and/or their family members" (p. 1512). The ministers talked about not being formally trained but using counseling that was Biblically based involving active listening. This study lends credence to the need to acknowledge formal and informal means of counseling. The ministers, recognizing their own limitations, also mentioned being able to connect mental health resources to older congregants.

In another study, the role of ministers in health equity was explored. Lumpkins et al. (2013) interviewed ministers about their beliefs regarding the promotion of health in their congregation through screening, sermons, and other issues; most of them were 60 and older and had attended health training workshops. Many led Baptist churches ranging from small (50 congregants) to large (1,000-plus members) and they told personal stories of health challenges to encourage congregants to take care of their own health and get screened. Other themes emerging from this research included (1) getting a sense of congregants' health as a whole, (2) understanding the relationship between spirituality, religion, and health, and (3) having a health ministry. A bonus theme was that of advocating for better access to health care and nutritious food such as affordable fruits and vegetables.

While some researchers have asked questions of ministers about what they do with their congregants regarding health, other studies have done so for parents. McBride (2013) asked parents whose average age was 52 how they would like to see the Black church impact their children. Over half of the parents were married, mostly women, and attended church more than once a week. Their focus group interviews yielded concepts such as values and communication as foundational to including spirituality/religious beliefs into a family health program. Other values included faith, love, prayer, respect, and community. They believed that these were all virtues that should be taught.

For older African-descended populations, coping strategies include religious coping. Holt et al. (2014) examined its relationship to fruit/vegetable consumption, smoking behavior, and alcohol use among African Americans whose average age was 53. Over half of them had some college and almost half were working. The researchers distinguished between religious behaviors and religious beliefs, as well as positive and negative religious coping. Both religious beliefs and religious behaviors were related to positive religious coping. Religious behaviors were negatively correlated with alcohol and tobacco use. Positive religious coping was positively correlated with vegetable intake and mediated the relationship between religious behaviors and vegetable intake.

In another study, Debnam et al. (2012) assessed this relationship and found that an active spiritual health locus of control predicted daily fruit consumption and less alcohol intake. The active spiritual health locus of control is the belief one has that the Creator gives them the power to take charge of their health. The opposite, if you will, is the belief that one does not have to do anything to take care of themselves because God is in control; this was seen as a passive spiritual health locus of control. Passive spiritual health locus of control predicted less daily vegetable consumption. Not only did the researchers find that there were no gender differences on spiritual health locus of control, but also the participants reported a more active spiritual health locus of control, compared to the passive spiritual health locus of control. The study's participants had an average age of 54, and almost half had completed a year of college.

Many Black people involved with the church believe that faith will keep away mental health challenges. For instance, participants in a study by Akinyemi et al. (2018) reported that if they prayed first, then feelings of depression were less likely to get worse. Their research involved participants ranging in age from 50 to 94; the average age of men was 59 while the average age of women was 67. There were gender differences between men and women on how they perceived depression. While men said "not wanting to eat" and "sleeping a lot" in line with characteristics of depression according to the DSM, women made no mention of it at all. The rest of the DSM criteria was addressed. Could it be that older men have a more complete picture of how depression looks, compared to women? Perhaps. But only one man supplied that answer. Although the researchers asked about the role of the church in "depression care," they did not report how the participants answered that question.

## EMOTIONAL WELL-BEING

Depressive symptoms have been exacerbated among the elderly as the COVID-19 pandemic lingers, especially in the United States. Although we previously discussed intervention programs, among the elderly, since our focus is on care, we will also discuss one program designed to tackle depression. Gitlin and colleagues (2014) examined a home-based program, Beat the Blues, designed for older adults of African descent. The average age of the participants was 69; they were mostly women with material resource challenges. Anxiety, depression knowledge, and behavioral activation all served as mediators between the Beat the Blues program and depressive symptoms. The researchers suggested that "our results lend strong support to multicomponent, nondrug approaches that help low-income older African Americans address the contextual factors impinging on their mood" (p. 608). This brings me to another thought. Many of the psychotropic drugs are not safe for elderly people, considering medication that they may be taking for physical ailments. The possibility of interaction effects cannot be ignored. Intervention programs, such as Beat the Blues and others, contribute to healthy ways to treat our elderly.

Emotional well-being's relationship to physical well-being cannot be devalued. In one study assessing emotional well-being among African Americans whose average age was 51, most of whom had finished high school, Warren-Findlow et al. (2011) found that it was predicted by family emotional support, friend emotional support, and good/excellent physical health. However, being partnered and experiencing daily discrimination translated to less-than-optimal emotional health, although friend/family emotional support served to mitigate racial discrimination. Friends and family are crucial to empowerment for older Black people as long as they are providing some type of support.

Body image among Black women has been studied by various researchers, some of whom have been puzzled as to why African-descended women tend to be more accepting of their physical structure, even though it does not often fit the European ideal of thinness. African American women whose average age was 75, most of whom were college graduates and widowed, completed measures related to satisfaction with body shape/function, BMI, general health, and mental health, among other variables. Sabik and Versey (2016) reported positive relationships between satisfaction with body shape and general health. Negative correlations were reported between satisfaction with body shape and BMI. Additionally, satisfaction with body shape/function predicted experiences of pain.

Racial discrimination affects African-descended people across the life span, and those who are older are no different. Among Black participants (60% women with an average age of 50), Moody et al. (2019) reported almost 40% experienced discrimination at work; 31% of them reported this phenomenon while getting a job, and the third most common way to experience this was getting discriminated against by police or in courts. The relationship between white matter lesion volume and discrimination was most evident for those over 60 and is important to note as it determines brain health.

Health outcomes related to telomere lengths have also been investigated among older Black people. For instance, Lee et al. (2017) reported discrimination experiences among participants with an average age of 70, most of whom never or used to smoke and exercised at least once a month. They found a relationship between discrimination and telomere length in that it was shortest for those experiencing the most discrimination.

Studies noting no gender or class differences among people of African descent seem to be quite common. It is interesting that race matters in a social context continue to impact health despite their non-biological basis. One study did report gender differences. Coley et al. (2017) examined discrimination and health related quality of life, among other variables. The average age of their sample was close to 73 and nearly half of them were married. There were gender differences in physically and mentally unhealthy days with women reporting more of those than men. Discrimination was related to poor health related quality of life and the relationship was stronger among women compared to men.

Resilience is a common refrain among older Black people. There are some studies however that indicate that it may not be enough to buffer discrimination, despite the negative correlation between the two variables observed in a study by Nadimpalli et al. (2015). The participants (mostly women) had an average age of 73 years. The researchers reported a positive correlation between discrimination and depression.

It seems that much of the research conducted regarding discrimination does not seem to consider cultural values in their analysis. Throughout the pandemic, I have had to constantly stress to well-meaning people that African-descended populations are more than their pain. I am beginning to understand why others reduce Black people to their experiences of racial discrimination; the literature seems to be replete with it. Missing from much of this research are cultural factors which would give one a more complete picture of this population.

## CAN YOU HEAR ME NOW?

A common theme among the elderly, regarding the relationship with their health care provider is that of problems with communication. Older Black men described these issues with their doctors, indicating that their physicians had challenges with understanding them (Hawkins & Mitchell, 2018). All of the men were over 60 years of age. The researchers compared those who said their doctors never listened with those who said they listened sometimes/ usually or always. They reported that mostly married or partnered men indicated doctors did listen. The opposite pattern appeared for those who said the doctor never listened; those who were widowed, separated, or divorced most often reported that the doctor never listened. This was a significant predictor of having a doctor who never listened, in addition to having limited moderate activity, challenges with their emotional health, and being older than 75.

It seems that being married or partnered would protect these elderly men against being ignored by the doctor. It is possible that having someone other than the patient to be accountable to might make a difference in the doctor's behavior. For older unpartnered African-descended men with children, it would be a good idea for a son or daughter (or close friend) to accompany them to the doctor to advocate for them just in case they cannot do so for themselves. This has implications for older Black unpartnered women, too. Having a younger relative such as a son, daughter, niece, or nephew to ensure that the doctor is treating the patient respectfully would be beneficial for all parties involved. Finally, while Hawkins and Mitchell (2018) did not ask the race of the doctors, it is possible that it might have made a difference in communication perceptions.

In another study, communication between medical personnel and their patients was explored. Song et al. (2012) studied participants who were breast cancer (average age of 60) and prostate cancer patients (average age of 67). Four themes emerged from the study. They included "communication of cancer information, communication of shared decision making, communication of empathy and understanding, and communication of respect." Most of the participants discussed the lack of shared decision making due to not knowing enough about cancer, as well as doctors pressuring them into options presented to them. The nagging feeling that they were not given the full range of options plagued the participants. Song et al. (2012) reported differences in communication between prostate cancer patients and breast cancer patients. Reading the comments of the prostate cancer patients was discouraging. But we should examine their reporting so that health care providers can know what not to do, such as not leaving messages about cancer on voicemail or addressing patients by their last names, a prime example of respect in the Black community.

Communication between health care practitioners and patients is key to health promotion. But before we get to the doctor, it is important to know about the family's health history so that we can better navigate our own health. Hovick et al. (2015) studied communication patterns about health among older African American and African participants whose average age was 74; most of them were in good health or better. The patterns the researchers observed fell into four types: "noncommunication (do not talk about health), open communication (talk about health), selective communication (tell some things about health), and one-way communication (lack of reciprocity)."

This cursory overview for empowering older African-descended populations should be a good starting point for those wishing to work with them.

Opening lines of communication is key. I frequently recommend that younger people ask older people to tell them their life story. We did that as children, and it is a good way to discuss topics related not just to health but cultural transmission imparted by the elders.

# Chapter 7

# Toward a Brighter Day

What is the future of health psychology as it relates to African-descended populations? Can we have a viable version of health psychology that does not include Black people? Can we have effective Africana studies programs that do not address the health psychology of African-descended populations? For one, we need for health psychology to be culturally grounded if we hope to effect change in these populations. Intervention programs that are culturally grounded can be found in communities around the world.

Self-testing for various diseases is part of the wave of the future. Community-based HIV self-testing was found to be effective among people in South Africa. Not only was it cost-effective for women who were sex workers, but also adult men (aged 25–49) were most likely to benefit in that subsequent HIV infections and AIDS deaths were avoided (Cambiano et al., 2019).

As we know this about HIV testing, a lesson could be taken for testing for COVID-19. To what extent would it be easier to allow for COVID-19 testing among Black people that does not require them to leave their homes? If they rely on public transportation, that has not been considered in the development of drive-through testing sites. Can we do self-testing for COVID-19 using World Health Organization's immediate results protocol? I asked these questions two years ago and here we are. Although the U.S. government has provided four testing kits per household, problems were evident in that Black, Indigenous, and people of color (BIPOC) were likely to have more people in their households than four. Additionally, residents were to request the kits online. Yet, what about if one does not have access to a computer or the internet?

## BLACK PEOPLE CAN'T GET COVID

When COVID-19 first appeared, there were rumors that Black people could not get it. Those were fueled by not just Black people who knew no one who had it, but also international communities such as the Chinese. In Guangzhou, China, where the African population is so large that there is a section of town called Africatown, the Afro beats club only shut down for 1 week at the height of the worldwide pandemic.

As time went on, the health equity challenges that we often discuss started to emerge. Populations of African descent were disproportionately being affected by COVID-19 in the United States. While people of African descent make up 13% of the U.S. population, they were 20% of the cases. In St. Louis, Missouri, at first, no one had recovered, and all the victims were African descended. How did it go from "Black people don't get COVID" to "Black people are disproportionately affected"?

The former head of the American Public Health Association, Dr. Camara Jones, explained that structural racism was responsible. Lack of access to health care is the number-one reason, in the only industrialized country without universal health care. The inability to access health care is due to full-time jobs being tied to health insurance and part-time jobs preventing its accessibility. The surgeon general and others wrongly attributed COVID-19 to race. The prominent narrative changed to if you are Black, you are more likely to get the virus.

The problem with the race equals COVID narrative is that it ignores class differences and even health differences. A person who is African descended in good health is not likely to succumb to the disease. Those with health issues such as a compromised immune system, diabetes, high blood pressure, and heart disease are more likely to get it, and this goes against racial lines. Dorothy Roberts' TED Talk is a must-watch regarding the medical industry's continuing reliance on race as a guide, as mentioned in an earlier chapter.

Media outlets repeated such narratives without an analytical perspective. It does not help that the former surgeon general, Jerome Adams, remarked that Black people were more likely to get COVID, so they (and Latinos) need to stop drinking alcohol, smoking tobacco, and doing drugs. He then went on to mention structural causes for the disproportionate representation among people of African descent. However, the first narrative, which blames the victims is flashier and fits the story of Black people in the United States as less than others.

## "TWINDEMIC"

For several months, some public health officials have recognized both COVID-19 and racism as pandemics. Although the term "twindemic" refers to the possibility of COVID-19 and the flu coexisting as pandemics, many health professionals have borrowed the term to refer to both the existence of COVID-19 and racism disproportionately affecting communities of African descent.

Even with marches in the wake of the George Floyd murder, which sparked protest around the world, the data indicated that the spike in COVID was not attributed to the largest mass movement in the history of the United States. Several people wore masks and attempted to physically distance themselves from others. Recent science has shown that the chances of catching COVID-19 decrease if one was outside.

The number of people killed by police compounded with state responses to mental health crises spurred some protesters to suggest that city governments defund the police. Over the past 40 years, almost half of city budgets have been allocated to policing at the expense of services to people which would alleviate the burden on police officers in the first place. The Minneapolis City Council is emblematic of some cities who decided to examine their police budgets; they reallocated $7.7 million of the $179 million Minneapolis Police Department budget for social services related needs. Yet, they still found a way to give the money back by allowing $11.4 million to exist in reserve. The city of Austin was more successful in allocating money to social services from the police department. In many ways, it would remove the social worker function of officers who did not sign up for that. A total of $870 million had been reallocated as of May 2021 across the country. It is unclear how much of the money has been given back to law enforcement.

Even when we know how to navigate the medical system, people of African descent still suffer negative outcomes. For instance, the belief that Black people can withstand a great amount of pain continues to persist as an outgrowth of slavery's past history which included medical experimentation. It was evidenced in the news of a Black doctor in Indiana who died from COVID-19. The white doctor "tending" to her discounted her need for medication to alleviate her pain. Dr. Susan Moore made a Facebook video regarding how she was being mistreated by doctors and nurses at the hospital she was in, eventually dying due to lack of care.

## VACCINE IMAGERY

How have health-promoting behaviors exhibited by Black populations been affected by the pandemic? The first person to take the COVID-19 vaccine was an African Caribbean (Jamaican) nurse working at Long Island Jewish Medical Center, Sandra Lindsay. Dr. Michelle Chester, also a Black woman, gave her the Pfizer vaccine. Another person of African descent, Dr. Kizzmekia Corbett, led the team of researchers who developed the Moderna vaccine. People of African descent taking the lead, knowing that their respective communities are more likely to be negatively impacted, is in line with the culture of care that continues, as a form of health promotion.

Due to previous (and current) abuses, cultural mistrust among Black people has ensued when it comes to a myriad of issues, but particularly with the health care system. Taken together, however, it is possible that spotlighting Dr. Corbett's role in the development of the vaccine may make Black people feel more comfortable about receiving it. That belief is what propelled medical officials to encourage people of African descent to get the vaccine.

It is likely that many African countries wanting the patent from Moderna/Pfizer, rather than taking the vaccine, may be due to the ugly history of Pfizer's vaccine harm regarding meningitis. The infrastructure can make the vaccine, but continued variations of COVID-19 will continue as long as Western countries refuse to share the patent and throw away vaccines which have expired. For Nigerians with long memories, the appearance of a vaccine by Pfizer may be triggering and possibly traumatizing (Garba & Abidakun, 2021).

Not only is there vaccine hesitancy among African-descended populations but also there is vaccine hesitancy in a different mode among the European Union. It has a vaccine passport system, but their hesitancy lies in its failure to include Covishield, the Indian version of AstraZeneca. The African Union and the African Center for Disease Control and Prevention protested this decision (Edward-Ekpu, 2021). Covishield had been distributed in Asian countries, such as India, as well as some African countries, and the patent had already been approved by the E.U. (BBC, 2021). The vaccine hesitancy by the E.U. has been of those vaccines not made by Europeans or the United States.

## TECHNOLOGY ADVANCEMENTS

In recent years, the use of apps has exploded to take care of mental health needs of Black people. Liberate and EXHALE, recently designed by a Black woman, Katara McCarty, are good places to start. The ancestor-guided-meditation part of it is rooted in culture. Although McCarty targets Black, Indigenous Women of Color, its focus on culture will take us a long way toward healing.

I was inspired to download apps related to tracking COVID. These, too, are the future and could possibly keep us safe. According to the COVID-19 Tracker app, my location in blue is surrounded by dots confirmed by the World Health Organization: red dots (confirmed positive COVID cases) and black dots (deaths due to COVID). The COVID-19 Tracker app keeps data on global cases, deaths, and recoveries, in addition to news, feeds, and chats. The other app I found useful is called CoVis; it estimates one's risk of COVID after entering demographic and health data.

## MORE BLACK DOCTORS

It remains to be seen whether the surge in Black applicants to medical school will translate into a surge in the number of Black doctors. The twindemic has led to an increase in the number of Black applicants to medical school. They range from 26% at Morehouse School of Medicine to 43% at the medical school at Texas Tech. There are two factors that may have led to this: virtual interviews and the waiver of the MCAT, typically depressing BIPOC applicants in general (Brown, 2021). In response to the Black Lives Matter protests, statements in support of Black lives were promoted by a majority of medical schools. However, if they meant for those statements alone to bring in future Black doctors, they will have to do more than that. Fewer than half of them had a targeted plan for diversifying their medical students. In order to sustain the increase in Black medical school students, a program for recruitment and retention ultimately has to be implemented (Jaschik, 2021).

Dr. Camara Jones and Dr. Joia Crear Perry drew a relationship between the death of George Floyd and the death of Dr. Susan Moore. They were two of four Black doctors who wrote an article in the *Washington Post* about it. The discussion about the twindemic ensued to form the foundation for the article. While police violence killed Mr. Floyd, the medical industry killed Dr. Moore. The common thread they shared was a blatant disregard for Black life (Democracy Now, 2020).

The mortality rate of Black women having a child has grown over the past 20 years (Sgaier & Downey, 2021). Things are supposed to be getting better, not worse. Issues such as these are the reason that many Black people see progress as a mixed bag. However, there is hope.

## MORE HOPE

A possible increase in Black doctors can have a beneficial effect on Black mothers and their babies. Researchers found that Black infants had an increased chance of survival if their doctors were Black. Greenwood et al. (2020) examined records of hospitals in Florida between 1992 and 2015 to see if equity existed between Black and white newborns, and whether it was related to the race of the doctor. They found that Black babies were three times less likely to live if the doctor was white. Mortality dropped by 58% when the doctor was Black. The researchers also examined maternal mortality and found the rate among Black mothers was three times that of white mothers; the race of the physician made no difference in that case, however (Greenwood et al., 2020).

If the infant survival rate differs due to race, it is possible that the missing link might be the cultural link. Maybe this effect was not evident among mothers because it was not just about race. Perhaps, if there was a cultural match between the mother and the doctor, the same effect might have been evident. As a reminder, culture and race are not interchangeable. Greenwood et al. (2020) also suggested that it is not feasible to choose a Black doctor all the time, hence the need for white doctors to be culturally competent.

The implicit bias in the medical profession makes one wonder if part of the impetus behind reformulating the MCAT was the knowledge that it is not enough to know the medicine alone. Health care providers have to be able to connect with their patients by understanding psychology and the other social sciences.

Government assistance is necessary for people of African descent in the diaspora to thrive. For instance, the Black Maternal Health Momnibus Act, proposed by U.S. lawmakers, would ensure that structural changes are targeted to enhance health equity, among other suggestions (Black Maternal Health Caucus, 2021). In line with the Neighborhood Voice mobile unit described by Alcaraz et al. (2011) earlier, there is a mobile unit provided for HIV intervention in Atlanta, supplemented by government funding. On the back of the van is the website www.standup2hivatl.org. Hence the need for government intervention, since government intervention created the problems of inequality in the first place.

The power of churches cannot be minimized during this pandemic. Some church congregations were told by their religious leaders not to get the vaccine, but they did require masks when churches did reopen. They have a huge amount of influence over their congregants.

There are two events that came out of the pandemic that tell us that Black people will take care. One is Club Quarantine, started by DJ D-Nice in March of 2020 as everything started to shut down. He no doubt provided a public service and as music is a healer, contributed to our ability to withstand the devastation inflicted on African-descended communities. The second are the Verzuz which brought friendly competitions often turning into lovefests including the likes of Erykah Badu v. Jill Scott and Musiq Soulchild v. Anthony Hamilton. The commentaries provided by the artists, in addition to singing/rapping or playing their songs, were a treat.

Is it possible that studies that take place in Africa might be automatically cultural anyway? Or does the impact of colonialism require a differentially conceptualized version of ethnic identity? This is an area of research to be considered for future studies, especially as they continue to evolve in health care among various African countries. The same might be considered for the Caribbean, South America, and other locales where Black people are the majority.

## RECOVERY ROAD

Race, migration, and gender are suggested as intersectional ways to describe COVID recovery experiences for African-descended populations in Canada by Etowa and Hyman (2021). This is emblematic of the lack of racial data collected by Canadian officials in the first place, but they suggested that they have had greater economic, personal, and health challenges compared to the majority of Canadians.

I did a session called "Cell Therapy" (a nod to Goodie Mob) to discuss self-care for mostly people of color working for a university. They enjoyed it and not only did we focus on brain cells (mental health), we also focused on cells in general (physical health) and feelings about being in a "cell." My focus on the positive and building resilience was more helpful at that moment, compared to pathologizing Black people in those moments.

A lot of what I brought into the session was based on research, some of which needs to be expanded to African-descended populations. For instance, the finding by Harvard researchers with an all-white sample was that those who meditated experienced brain growth, and other positive outcomes including emotional well-being. My colleague said it was good because she thought a lot of her staff were sad. A large part of getting through this process is cell therapy, including limited social media and news intake, as the focus is on "if it bleeds, it leads." A brief discussion about cutting out sugar, as a major source of disease, ensued. I suggested limiting snacks to once a day. An increase in fruits/vegetables and decrease in meats was also proffered. I emphasized the "me times for mommies" without scaring them that life would be shorter without it.

During the pandemic, HBCUs have continued the tradition of providing services to the community in line with some of their earlier health promotion activities, mentioned in chapter 2. Some offered everything from testing to vaccinations. Others joined with PWIs (predominantly white institutions) to conduct research (Patterson, 2021). The researcher suggested that the key to advocating for health equity in communities of African descent should consider scientists at HBCUs as they often have their fingers on the pulse of its heartbeat.

## EPILOGUE

As I put the finishing touches on this book, I have had an adventure trying to get a COVID test. The home testing kit indicated a negative result, but it may have been because it was too soon to test. We recently learned that the kits' accuracy is in question, and the best determination would be to get a PCR (polymerase chain reaction) test. It took three days to get a PCR test. On day 1, I was told I had to register for it; appointments were not available for almost a week with Walgreens and CVS. I had been on the state health department's website, which directed me back to the drugstores. A friend in another state directed me to the county health department's website. There were two locations listed, and I registered with one at the church, as the county's location contained no directions for registering. On day 2, we went to the church to be turned away due to inclement weather. On day 3, the testing location was closed, so we ventured to the county health department, where we finally took the test.

## A CHANGE IS GONNA COME

Future research directions and suggestions for the health equity for African-descended populations throughout the diaspora should be evaluated for effectiveness (or lack thereof). The focus should be on a collective responsibility, one of the values noted in an earlier chapter. All these systems must work together, according to Kidanemariam (2011), and he provides the example of Uganda and Rwanda as having interlocking systems which have ensured the health of its residents.

In the early days of the pandemic, researchers called for culturally sensitive perspectives for treating those affected, many of whom were Black people. Airhihenbuwa et al. (2020) suggested that the PEN-3 cultural model should be used by health practitioners; this was discussed in a previous chapter. Community could be best served by considering culture, according to the researchers, in addition to individual variables. Scientists have warned that there will be future pandemics and we could best meet the needs of the most vulnerable by considering their culture.

Telemedicine has come a long way since the pandemic began. Many health care professionals from psychologists to physicians continue to see their patients through electronic means. In some ways, it has contributed to health equity. For instance, Bressman et al. (2022) reported that telemedicine played an integral role in enabling Black patients to follow up with their doctors after being discharged from the hospital.

Core cultural values of African descended people have been outlined in this book. Collectivism, spirituality, resilience, social support, and the community of care were evident in the review and interpretation of research presented. My hope is that we can move toward promoting health for Black communities in a way that considers their culture. You now have the tools necessary to do so.

# References

Adams, R. D., & Johnson, W. E., Jr. (2021). Faith as a mechanism for health promotion among rural African American prostate cancer survivors: A qualitative examination. *International Journal of Environmental Research and Public Health, 18*, 3134–3151. https://doi.org/10.3390/ijerph18063134

Ahn, L. H., Dunbar, A. S., Coates, E. E., & Smith-Bynum, M. A. (2021). Cultural and university parenting, ethnic identity, and internalizing symptoms among African American adolescents. *Journal of Black Psychology, 47*(8), 695–717.

Airhihenbuwa, C., Iwelunmor, J., Munodawafa, D., Ford, C., Oni, T., Agyemang, C., Mota, C., Ikuomola, O., Simbayi, L., Fallah, M., Qian, Z., Makinwa, B., Niang, C., & Okosun, I. (2020). Culture matters in communicating the global response to COVID-19. *Preventing Chronic Disease, 17*(60), 1–8. https://doi.org/10.5888/pcd17.200245

Airhihenbuwa, C. O., & Liburd, L. (2006). Eliminating health disparities in the African American population: The interface of culture, gender, and power. *Health Education and Behavior, 33*(4), 488–501.

Ajibade, P. B. (2011). Physical activity patterns by campus housing status among African American female college students. *Journal of Black Studies, 42*(4), 548–560. DOI: 10.1177/0021934710385116

Akinwumi, O. (2006). Youth participation in violence in Nigeria since the 1980s. In C. Daiute, Z. Beykont, C. Higson-Smith, & L. Nucci (Eds.), *International perspectives on youth conflict and development* (pp. 73–85). Oxford University Press.

Akinyemi, E., Watkins, D. C., Kavanaugh, J., Johnson-Lawrence, V., Lynn, S., & Kales, H. C. (2018). A qualitative comparison of DSM depression criteria to language used by older church-going African Americans. *Aging and Mental Health, 22*(9), 1149–1155. https://doi.org/10.1080/13607863.2017.1337717

Alcaraz, K. I., Weaver, N. L., Andresen, E. M., Christopher, K., & Kreuter, M. W. (2011). The Neighborhood Voice: Evaluating a mobile research vehicle for recruiting African Americans to participate in cancer control studies. *Evaluation and the Health Professions, 34*(3), 336–348.

Alexander, D. S., Alfonso, M. L., & Hansen, A. R. (2015). Childhood obesity perceptions among African American caregivers in a rural Georgia community: A mixed methods approach. *Journal of Community Health, 40*, 367–378. DOI:10.1007/s10900-014-9945-4

Algood, C., & Davis, A. M. (2019). Inequities in family quality of life for African American families raising children with disabilities. *Social Work in Public Health, 34*(1), 102–112. https://doi.org/10.1080/19371918.2018.1562399

Allen, J. D., Akinyemi, I. C., Reich, A., Fleary, S., Tendulkar, S., & Lamour, N. (2018). African American women's involvement in promoting informed decision-making for prostate cancer screening among their partners/spouses. *American Journal of Men's Health, 12*(4), 884–893. DOI:10.1177/1557988317742257

Alvarado, M., Murphy, M. M., & Guell, C. (2015). Barriers and facilitators to physical activity amongst overweight and obese women in an Afro-Caribbean population: A qualitative study. *International Journal of Behavioral Nutrition and Physical Activity, 12*, 97–109. DOI: 10.1186/s12966-015-0258-5

Anderson, R. E., & Stevenson, H. C. (2019). RECASTing racial stress and trauma: Theorizing the healing potential of racial socialization in families. *American Psychologist, 74*(1), 63–75. http://dx.doi.org/10.1037/amp0000392

Anderson, R. E., McKenny, M., Mitchell, A., Koku, L., & Stevenson, H. C. (2018). EMBRacing racial stress and trauma: Preliminary feasibility and coping responses of a racial socialization intervention. *Journal of Black Psychology, 44*(1), 25–46. DOI: 10.1177/0095798417732930

Arnold, E. A., Kegeles, S. M., Pollack, L. M., Neilands, T. B., Cornwell, S. M., Steward, W. R., Benjamin, M., Weeks, J., Lockett, G., Smith, C. D., & Operario, D. (2019). A randomized controlled trial to reduce HIV-related risk in African American men who have sex with men and women: The Bruthas Project. *Prevention Science, 20*, 115–125. https://doi.org/10.1007/s11121-018-0965-7

Arsenault, C. E., Fisher, S., Stevens-Watkins, D., & Barnes-Najor, J. (2018). The indirect effect of ethnic identity on marijuana use through school engagement: An African American high school sample. *Substance Use and Misuse, 53*(9), 1444–1453. https://doi.org/10.1080/10826084.2017.1412464

Asare, M., Okafor, C. N., & Bautista, K. J. (2020). Assessment of perceptions and impacts of COVID-19, and adherence to public health recommendation among Black/African Americans. *American Journal of Health Studies, 35*(4), 270–285.

Aymer, S. R. (2016). "I can't breathe": A case study—helping Black men cope with race-related trauma stemming from police killings and brutality. *Journal of Human Behavior in the Social Environment, 26*, 367–376. http://dx.doi.org/10.1080/1091 1359.2015.1132828

Baldwin, J. A. (1979). Theory and research concerning the notion of Black self-hatred: A review and reinterpretation. *Journal of Black Psychology, 5*(2), 51–77.

Baldwin, J. A., & Bell, Y. R. (1985). The African self-consciousness scale: An Africentric personality questionnaire. *The Western Journal of Black Studies, 9*(2), 61–68.

Banks, D. E., Riley, T. N., Bernard, D. L., Fisher, S., & Barners-Najor, J. (2021). Traditional risk and cultural protection: Correlates of alcohol and cannabis co-use among African American adolescents. *Psychology of Addictive Behaviors, 35*(6), 671–681.

Banks, K. H., & Kohn-Wood, L. (2007). The influence of racial identity profiles on the relationship between racial discrimination and depressive symptoms. *Journal of Black Psychology, 33*(3), 331–354.

Banks, K. H., & Stephens, J. (2018). Reframing internalized racial oppression and charting a way forward. *Social Issues and Policy Review, 12*(1), 91–111.

Barbarin, O. A. (1983). Coping with ecological transitions by Black families: A psychosocial model. *Journal of Community Psychology, 11*(4), 308–322.

Barr, S., & Neville, H. (2014). Racial socialization, color-blind racial ideology, and mental health among Black college students: An examination of an ecological model. *Journal of Black Psychology, 40*, 138–165.

BBC. (2021, July 1). *Covishield: Seven EU countries approve India's COVID vaccines.* https://www.bbc.com/news/world-asia-india-57628123

Beach, S. R. H., Lei, M. K., Brody, G. H., Yu, T., & Philibert, R. A. (2014). Nonsupportive parenting affects telomere length in young adulthood among African Americans: Mediation through substance use. *Journal of Family Psychology, 28*(6), 967–972.

Beagan, B. L., & Chapman, G. E. (2012). Meaning of food, eating, and health among African Nova Scotians: "Certain things aren't meant for Black folk." *Ethnicity and Health, 17*(5), 513–529.

Beatty, L., Wheeler, D., & Gaiter, J. (2004). HIV prevention research for African Americans: Current and future directions. *Journal of Black Psychology, 30*(1), 40–58. DOI: 10.1177/0095798403259245

Bediako, S. M., Lavender, A. R., & Yasin, Z. (2007). Racial centrality and health care use among African American adults with sickle cell disease. *Journal of Black Psychology, 33*(4), 422–438.

Belgrave, F. Z., Marin, B. V. O., & Chambers, D. B. (2000). Cultural, contextual, and intrapersonal predictors of risky sexual attitudes among urban African American girls in early adolescence. *Cultural Diversity and Ethnic Minority Psychology, 6*(3), 309–322.

Black Maternal Health Caucus. (2021). *Black Maternal Health Momnibus.* https://blackmaternalhealthcaucus-underwood.house.gov/Momnibus

Bliss, M. J., Ogley-Oliver, E., Jackson, E., Harp, S., & Kaslow, N. (2008). African American women's readiness to change abusive relationships. *Journal of Family Violence, 23*, 161–171. DOI: 10.1007/s10896-007-9138-3

Blum, R. W., Halcon, L., Beuhring, T., Pate, E., Campbell-Forrester, S., & Venema, A. (2003). Adolescent health in the Caribbean: Risk and protective factors. *American Journal of Public Health, 93*, 456–460.

Bressman, E., Werner, R. M., Childs, C., Albrecht, A., Myers, J. S., & Adusumalli, S. (2022). Association of telemedicine with primary care appointment access after hospital discharge. *Journal of General Internal Medicine.* DOI: 10.1007/s11606-021-0732103

Brittain, K., & Murphy, V. P. (2015). Sociocultural and health correlates related to colorectal cancer screening adherence among urban African Americans. *Cancer Nursing, 38*(2), 118–124.

Brody, G. H., Yu, T., Chen, E., Ehrlich, K. B., & Miller, G. E. (2018). Racial discrimination, body mass index, and insulin resistance: A longitudinal analysis. *Health Psychology, 37*(12), 1107–1114. https://doi.org/10.1037/hea0000674

Brody, G., Yu, T., Chen, E., & Miller, G. E. (2020). Persistence of skin-deep resilience in African American adults. *Health Psychology, 39*(10), 921–926.

Brody, G., Yu, T., Chen, Y., Kogan, S., & Smith, K. (2012). The Adults in the Making Program: Long-term protective stabilizing effects on alcohol use and substance use problems for rural African American emerging adults. *Journal of Consulting and Clinical Psychology, 80*, 17–28.

Bronder, E. C., Speight, S. L., Witherspoon, K. M., & Thomas, A. J. (2014). John Henryism, depression, and perceived social support in Black women. *Journal of Black Psychology, 40*, 115–137. DOI: 10.1177/0095798412474466

Brown, D. (2021, February 11). *There's been a surge in Black medical school applicants amid COVID's devastation.* Blavity. https://blavity.com/theres-been-a-surge-in-black-medical-school-applicants-amid-covids-devastation-on-bipoc-communities?category1=news

Bryant, W. W. (2011). Internalized racism's association with African American male youth's propensity for violence. *Journal of Black Studies, 42*(4), 690–707.

Butler-Barnes, S. T., Martin, P. P., Hope, E. C., Copeland-Linder, N., & Scott, M. L. (2018). Religiosity and coping: Racial stigma and psychological well-being among African American girls. *Journal of Religion and Health, 57*, 1980–1995.

Caldwell, C. H., Sellers, R. M., Bernat, D. H., & Zimmerman, M. A. (2004). Racial identity, parental support and alcohol use in a sample of academically at-risk African American high school students. *American Journal of Community Psychology, 34*(1/2), 71–82.

Cambiano, V., Johnson, C. C., Hatzold, K., Terris-Prestholt, F., Maheswaran, H., Thirumurthy, H., Figueroa, C., Cowan, F. M., Sibanda, E. L., Ncube, G., Revill, P., Baggaley, R. C., Corbett, E. L., and Phillips, A. (2019). The impact and cost-effectiveness of community-based HIV self-testing in sub-Saharan Africa: A health economic and modelling analysis. *Journal of the International AIDS Society, 22*, 82–93. https://doi.org/10.1002/jia2.25243

Campbell, C., Cornish, F., & Mclean, C. (2004). Social capital, participation and the perpetuation of health inequalities: Obstacles to African Caribbean participation in 'partnerships' to improve mental health. *Ethnicity and Health, 9*(4), 313–335.

Carter, S. E., Ong, M. L., Simons, R. L., Gibbons, F. X., Lei, M. K., & Beach, S. R. H. (2019). The effect of early discrimination on accelerated aging among African Americans. *Health Psychology, 38*(11), 1010–1013. https://doi.org/10.1037/hea0000788

Carter, S. E., & Walker, R. L. (2014). Anxiety symptomatology and perceived health in African American adults: Moderating role of emotion regulation. *Cultural Diversity and Ethnic Minority Psychology, 20*(3), 307–315.

Chae, D. H., Lincoln, K. D., & Jackson, J. S. (2011). Discrimination, attribution, and racial group identification: Implications for psychological distress among Black Americans in the National Survey of American Life, 2001–2003. *American Journal of Orthopsychiatry, 81*(4), 498–506.

Chae, D. H., Wang, Y., Martz, C. D., Slopen, N., Yip, T., Adler, N. E., Fuller-Rowell, T. E., Lin, J., Matthews, K. A., Brody, G. H., Spears, E. C., Puterman, E., & Epel, E. S. (2020). Racial discrimination and telomere shortening among African Americans: The Coronary Artery Risk Development in Young Adults (CARDIA) Study. *Health Psychology, 39*(3), 209–219. https://doi.org/10.1037/hea0000832

Chethik, M., Fleming, E., Mayer, M. F., & McCoy, J. N. (1967). A quest for identity: Treatment of disturbed Negro children in a predominately White treatment center. *American Journal of Orthopsychiatry*, 71–77.

Child, S. T., Kaczynski, A. T., Fair, M. L., Stowe, E. W., Hughey, S. M., Boeckermann, L., Wills, S., & Reeder, Y. (2019). "We need a safe, walkable way to connect our sisters and brothers": A qualitative study of opportunities and challenges for neighborhood-based physical activity among residents of low-income African American communities. *Ethnicity and Health, 24*(4), 353–364. https://doi.org/10.1080/13557858.2017.1351923

Chipungu, S. S., Hermann, J., Sambrano, S., Nistler, M., Sale, E., & Springer, J. F. (2000). Prevention programming for African American youth: A review of strategies in CSAP's national cross-site evaluation of high-risk youth programs. *Journal of Black Psychology, 26*(4), 360–385.

Christie-Mizell, C. A., Leslie, E. T. A., & Hearne, B. N. (2017). Self-related health, discrimination, and racial group identity: The consequences of ethnicity and nativity among Black Americans. *Journal of African American Studies, 21*, 643–664.

Claridy, M. D., Ansa, B., Damus, F., Alema-Mensah, E., & Smith, S. A. (2018). Health-related quality of life of African-American female breast cancer survivors, survivors of other cancers, and those without cancer. *Quality of Life Research, 27*, 2067–2075.

Clark, E. M., Williams, B. R., Huang, J., Roth, D. L., & Holt, C. L. (2018). A longitudinal study of religiosity, spiritual health locus of control, and health behaviors in a national sample of African Americans. *Journal of Religion and Health, 57*, 2258–2278.

Clubb, P. A., Browne, D. C., Humphrey, A. D., Schoenbach, V., Meyer, B., Jackson, & the RSVPP Steering Committee. (2001). Violent behaviors in early adolescent minority youth: Results from a "Middle School Youth Risk Behavior Survey." *Maternal and Child Health Journal, 5*, 225–235.

Coard, S. I., Wallace, S. A., Stevenson, H. C., Jr., & Brotman, L. M. (2004). Towards culturally relevant preventive interventions: The consideration of racial socialization in parent training with African Americans families. *Journal of Child and Family Studies, 13*(3), 277–293.

Cole, H., Thompson, H. S., White, M., Browne, R., Trinh-Shevrin, C., Braithwaite, S., Fiscella, K., Boutin-Foster, C., & Ravenell, J. (2017). Community-based, preclinical patient navigation for colorectal cancer screening among older Black men recruited from barbershops: The MISTER B Trial. *American Journal of Public Health, 107*(9), 1433–1440. DOI: 10.2105/AJPH.2017.303885

Coleman, M., Chapman, S., & Wang, D. (2012). An examination of color-blind racism and race-related stress among African American undergraduate students. *Journal of Black Psychology, 39*, 486–504.

Coley, S. L., de Leon, C. F. M., Ward, E. C., Barnes, L. L., Skarupski, K. A., & Jacobs, E. A. (2017). Perceived discrimination and health related quality of life: Gender differences among African Americans. *Quality of Life Research, 26*, 3449–3458. DOI: 10.1007/s11136-017–166309

Collins, P. H. (1990). *Black feminist thought: Knowledge, consciousness, and the politics of empowerment.* Routledge.

Cooley, C. H. (1902). Looking-glass self. In J. O'Brien (Ed.), *The production of reality: Essays and readings on social interaction,* (pp. 126–128). Sage.

Cooper Owens, D., & Fett, S. M. (2019). Black maternal and infant health: Historical legacies of slavery. *American Journal of Public Health, 109*(10), 1342–1345. DOI: 10.2105/AJPH.2019.305243

Corbie-Smith, G., Adimora, A., Youmans, S., Muhammad, M., Blumenthal, C., Ellison, A., Akers, A., Council, B., Thigpen, Y., Wynn, M., & Lloyd, S. (2011). Project GRACE: A staged approach to development of a community-academic partnership to address HIV in rural African American communities. *Health Promotion Practice, 12*(2), 293–302. DOI: 10.1177/1524839909348766

Cornely, P. B., & Alexander, V. M. (1939). The health status of the Negro in the United States. *The Journal of Negro Education, 8*(3), 359–375.

Corral, I., & Landrine, H. (2012). Racial discrimination and health-promoting vs damaging behaviors among African-American adults. *Journal of Health Psychology, 17*, 1176–1182.

Crenshaw, K. (1989). Demarginalizing the intersection of race and sex: A Black feminist critique of antidiscrimination doctrine, feminist theory, and antiracist politics. *University of Chicago Legal Forum*, 139–167.

Cross, W. E. (2003). Tracing the historical origins of youth delinquency and violence: Myths and realities about Black culture. *Journal of Social Issues, 59*(1), 67–82. https://doi.org/10.1111/1540-4560.t01-1-00005

Cunningham-Erves, J., Talbott, L. L., O'Neal, M. R., Ivankova, N. V., & Wallston, K. A. (2016). Development of a theory-based sociocultural instrument to assess Black maternal intentions to vaccinate their daughters aged 9–12 against HPV. *Journal of Cancer Education, 31*, 514–521. DOI: 10.1007/s13187-015-086703

Dale, S. K., & Safren, S. A. (2018). Resilience takes a village: Black women utilize support from their community to foster resilience against multiple adversities. *AIDS Care, 30*(S5), S18–S26. https://doi.org/10.1080/09540121.2018.1503225

Davis, G. Y., & Stevenson, H. C. (2006). Racial socialization experiences and symptoms of depression among Black youth. *Journal of Child and Family Studies, 15*(3), 303–317.

Debnam, K., Holt, C., Clark, E., Roth, D., Foushee, H., Crowther, M., Fouad, M., & Southward, P. (2012). Spiritual health locus of control and health behaviors in African Americans. *American Journal of Health Behavior, 36*, 360–372. DOI: http://dx.doi.org/10.5993/AJHB.36.3.7

DeJesus, M., Carrete, C., Maine, C., & Nalls, P. (2015). "Getting tested is almost like going to the Salem witch trials": Discordant discourses between Western public health messages and sociocultural expectations surrounding HIV testing among East African immigrant women. *AIDS Care, 27*(5), 604–611.

Democracy Now. (2020, December 30). *Say her name: Dr. Susan Moore. Black female doctors condemn racial disparities in healthcare.* https://www.democracynow.org/2020/12/30/joia_crear_perry_camara_phyllis_jones

DeNisco, S. (2011). Exploring the relationship between resilience and diabetes outcomes in African Americans. *Journal of the American Academy of Nurse Practitioners, 23*, 602–610.

Doran, J. (2004, November 30). *Guinea pig kids* [Video]. YouTube. https://www.youtube.com/watch?app=desktop&v=4K2Wp_WutVM

Drescher, C. F., Johnson, L. R., Kurz, A. S., Scales, P. C., & Kiliho, R. P. (2018). A Developmental Assets approach in East Africa: Can Swahili measures capture adolescent strengths and supports? *Child Youth Care Forum, 47*, 23–43. https://doi.org/10.1007/s10566-017-9415-0

Drolet, C. E., & Lucas, T. (2020). Perceived racism, affectivity, and C-reactive protein in healthy African Americans: Do religiosity and racial identity provide complementary protection? *Journal of Behavioral Medicine, 43*, 932–942. https://doi.org/10.1007/s10865-020-00146-1

Du Bois, W. E. B. (1899/1967). *The Philadelphia Negro: A social study.* Schocken Books.

Edward-Ekpu, U. (2021, July 4). *The EU's new vaccine passport is causing whiplash for Africans and Indians.* Quartz. https://qz.com/africa/2028738/can-africans-and-indians-use-europes-vaccine-passport-system/?utm_source=email&utm_medium=africa-weekly-brief&utm_content=5f52b417-e0ab-11eb-98fa-da5bfa9dc4ea

Eke, A. N., Johnson, W. D., O'Leary, A., Rebchook, G. M., Huebner, D. M., Peterson, J. L., & Kegeles, S. M. (2019). Effect of a community-level HIV prevention intervention on psychosocial determinants of HIV risk behaviors among young Black men who have sex with men (YBMSM). *AIDS and Behavior, 23*, 2361–2374. https://doi.org/10.1007/s10461-019-02499-4

Ellis, R. (2006, September 21). Cancer docs profit from chemotherapy drugs. *NBC News.* http://www.nbcnews.com/id/14944098/ns/nbc_nightly_news_with_brian_williams/t/cancer-docs-profit-chemotherapy-drugs

English, D., Carter, J. A., Forbes, N., Bowleg, L., Malebranche, D. J., Talan, A. J., & Rendina, H. J. (2020). Intersectional discrimination, positive feelings, and health indicators among Black sexual minority men. *Health Psychology, 39*(3), 220–229. https://doi.org/10.1037/hea0000837

Erikson, E. (1950). *Childhood and society.* W. W. Norton.

Erikson, E. (1968). *Identity: Youth and crisis.* W. W. Norton.

Etowa, J., & Hyman, I. (2021). Unpacking the health and social consequences of COVID-19 through a race, migration, and gender lens. *Canadian Journal of Public Health, 112*, 8–11. https://doi.org/10.17269/s41997-020-00456-6

Feleke, B. (2021, March 13). *Tanzania's prime minister dispels rumors about president Magufuli's health after COVID19 speculation.* CNN. https://www.cnn.com/2021/03/13/africa/magufuli-health-tanzania-intl/index.html

Fitzpatrick, K. M., Piko, B. F., Wright, D. R., & LaGory, M. (2005). Depressive symptomatology, exposure to violence, and the role of social capital among African American adolescents. *American Journal of Orthopsychiatry, 75*, 262–274.

Ford, C. L., & Airhihenbuwa, C. O. (2010). The public health critical race methodology: Praxis for antiracism research. *Social Science and Medicine, 71*, 1390–1398.

Forman, T. A. (2003). The social psychological costs of racial segmentation in the workplace: A study of African American well-being. *Journal of Health and Social Behavior, 44*(3), 332–352.

Fraser, M. W., & Richman, J. M. (2001). Resilience: Implications for evidence-based practice. In J. M. Richman & M. W. Fraser (Eds.), *The context of youth violence: Resilience, risk, and protection* (pp. 187–198). Praeger.

Frazier, E. F. (1925). Psychological factors in Negro health. *Journal of Social Forces, 3*(3), 488–490. https://doi.org/10.2307/3005007

Freeman, E. W., Rickels, K., Huggins, G. R., Mudd, E. H., Garcia, C., & Dickens, H. (1980). Adolescent contraceptive use: Comparisons of male and female attitudes and information. *American Journal of Public Health, 70*(8), 775–797. https://doi.org/10.2105/AJPH.70.8.790

French, S. E., Seidman, E., Allen, L., & Aber, J. L. (2006). The development of ethnic identity during adolescence. *Developmental Psychology, 42*, 1–10.

Fuller-Rowell, T. E., Cogburn, C. D., Brodish, A. B., Peck, S. C., Malanchuk, O., & Eccles, J. S. (2012). Racial discrimination and substance use: Longitudinal associations and identity moderators. *Journal of Behavioral Medicine, 35*, 581–590.

Galloway, J. (2020, January 12). Maternal death rate crisis will challenge lawmakers. *The Atlanta Journal-Constitution*, pp. B1, B6.

Gamble, V. N. (2016). "Outstanding Services to Negro Health": Dr. Dorothy Boulding Ferebee, Dr. Virginia M. Alexander, and Black women physicians' public health activism. *American Journal of Public Health, 106*(8), 1397–1404.

Garba, M., & Abidakun, M. (2021, July 12). *Vaccine hesitancy—The Pfizer Kano case*. Unbias the News. https://unbiasthenews.org/vaccination-hesitancy-the-pfizer-kano-case

Georgia State University Library Exhibits. (n.d.). *National Negro Health Week*. https://exhibits.library.gsu.edu/current/exhibits/show/health-is-a-human-right/healthcare-for-all/national-negro-health-week

Gibbons, F. X., Gerrard, M., Fleischli, M. E., Simons, R. L., & Kingsbury, J. H. (2021). Perceived racial discrimination and healthy behavior among African Americans. *Health Psychology, 40*(3), 155–165.

Gilbert, S. C., Crump, S., & Madhere, S., & Schutz, W. (2009). Internalization of the thin ideal as a predictor of body dissatisfaction and disordered eating in African, African American and Afro-Caribbean female college students. *Journal of College Student Psychotherapy, 23*, 196–211. DOI:10.1080/87568220902794093

Gillum, T. (2008). The benefits of a cultural specific intimate partner violence intervention for African American survivors. *Violence against Women, 14*(8), 917–943. DOI: 10.1177/1077801208321982

Gitlin, L. N., Roth, D. L., & Huang, J. (2014). Mediators of the impact of a home-based intervention (Beat the Blues) on depressive symptoms among older African Americans. *Psychology and Aging, 29*(3), 601–611.

Gittelsohn, J., Trude, A., Poirier, L., Ross, A., Ruggiero, C., Schwendler, T., & Steeves, E. A. (2017). The impact of a multi-level multi-component childhood obesity prevention intervention on healthy food availability, sales, and purchasing in a low-income urban area. *International Journal of Environmental Research and Public Health, 14*, 1371–1386. DOI: 10.3390/ijerph14111371

Gondolf, E. W., & Williams, O. J. (2001). Culturally focused batterer counseling for African American men. *Trauma, Violence, and Abuse, 2*, 283–295.

Goren, S. (2001). Healing the victim, the young offender, and the community via restorative justice: An international perspective. *Issues in Mental Health Nursing, 22*, 137–149.

Graham, J. R., West, L. M., Martinez, J., & Roemer, L. (2016). The mediating role of internalized racism in the relationship between racist experiences and anxiety symptoms in a Black American sample. *Cultural Diversity and Ethnic Minority Psychology, 22*(3), 369–376. https://doi.org/10.1037/cdp0000073

Gray, R. E., Fergus, K. D., & Fitch, M. I. (2005). Two Black men with prostate cancer: A narrative approach. *British Journal of Health Psychology, 10*(1), 71–84. https://doi.org/10.1348/135910704X14429

Greaney, M. L., Askew, S., Wallington, S. F., Foley, P. B., Quintiliani, L. M., & Bennett, G. G. (2017). The effect of a weight gain prevention intervention on moderate-vigorous physical activity among black women: the Shape Program. *International Journal of Behavioral Nutrition and Physical Activity, 14*, 1–8. DOI 10.1186/s12966-017-0596-6

Greenwood, B. N., Hardeman, R. R., Huang, L., & Sojourner, A. (2020). Physician–patient racial concordance and disparities in birthing mortality for newborns. *Proceedings of the National Academy of Sciences, 117*(35), 21194–21200. https://doi.org/10.1073/pnas.1913405117

Halgunseth, L. C., Jensen, A. C., Sakuma, K., & McHalem S. M. (2016). The role of mothers' and fathers' religiosity in African American adolescents' religious beliefs and practices. *Cultural Diversity and Ethnic Minority Psychology, 22*(3), 386–394.

Hannon, M. D., White, E. E., & Nadrich, T. (2018). Influence of autism on fathering style among Black American fathers: A narrative inquiry. *Journal of Family Therapy, 40*, 224–246. DOI: 10.1111/1467–6427.12165

Harrell, S. P. (1997, May). *Development and initial validation of scales to measure racism-related stress* [Paper presentation]. Presented at the 6th Biennial Conference on Community Research and Action, Society for Community Research and Action, Columbia, SC.

Harris, R. M., Rose, A. M.C., Soares-Wynter, S., & Unwin, N. (2021). Ultra-processed food consumption in Barbados: Evidence from a nationally representative, cross-sectional study. *Journal of Nutritional Science, 10*(29), 1–9.

Harvey, R. D., & Afful, S. E. (2011). Racial typicality, racial identity, and health behaviors: A case for culturally sensitive health interventions. *Journal of Black Psychology, 37*(2), 164–184. DOI: 10.1177/0095798410376244

Hawkins, J. M., & Mitchell, J. (2018). The doctor never listens: Older African American men's perceptions of patient-provider communication. *Social Work Research, 42*(1), 57–63.

Heads, A. M. B., Glover, A. M., Castillo, L. G., Blozis, S., & Kim, S. Y. (2018). Dimensions of ethnic identity as protective factors for substance use and sexual risk behaviors in African American college students. *Journal of American College Health, 66*(3), 178–186.

Hekler, E., Lambert, J., Leventhal, E., Leventhal, H., Jahn, E., & Contrada, R. (2008). Commonsense illness beliefs, adherence behaviors, and hypertension control among African Americans. *Journal of Behavioral Medicine, 31*, 391–400.

Hempstead, B., Green, C., Briant, K. J., Thompson, B., & Molina, Y. (2018). Community Empowerment Partners (CEPs): A breast health education program for African-American women. *Journal of Community Health, 43*(5), 833–841. doi:10.1007/s10900-018-0490-4

Henrickson, H., Crowther, J., & Harrington, E. F. (2010). Ethnic identity and maladaptive eating: Expectancies about eating and thinness in African American women. *Cultural Diversity and Ethnic Minority Psychology, 16*(1), 87–93.

Herd, D., & Grube, J. (1996). Black identity and drinking in the U.S.: A national study. *Addiction, 91*(6), 845–857.

Higginbottom, G. M. A. (2006). 'Pressure of life': Ethnicity was a mediating factor in mid-life and older peoples' experience of high blood pressure. *Sociology of Health and Illness, 28*(5), 583–610.

Holland, B. (2018, December 4). *The "father of modern gynecology" performed shocking experiments on enslaved women.* History Channel. https://www.history .com/news/the-father-of-modern-gynecology-performed-shocking-experiments-on -slaves

Holliday, R. C., Phillips, R., Akintobi, T. H., Mubasher, M., Banerjee, A., Hoffman, L., Walton, S., & Braithwaite, R. (2020). Project HAPPY: A community based participatory research intervention in Black youth. *American Journal of Health Studies, 35*(2), 93–101.

Holmes, G. R., & Heckel, R. V. (1970). Psychotherapy with the first Negro male on one southern university campus: A case study. *Journal of Consulting and Clinical Psychology, 34*(3), 297–301. https://doi.org/10.1037/h0029364

Holt, C. L., Clark, E. M., Debnam, K. J., & Roth, D. L. (2014). Religion and health in African Americans: The role of religious coping. *American Journal of Health Behavior, 38*(2), 190–199.

Hovick, S. R., Yamasaki, J. S., Burton-Chase, A. M., & Peterson, S. K. (2015). Patterns of family health history communication among older African American adults. *Journal of Health Communication, 20*, 80–87. DOI: 10.1080/10810730.2014.908984

Howard, D. (1996). Searching for resilience among African American youth exposed to community violence: Theoretical issues. *Journal of Adolescent Health, 18*, 254–262.

Hudson, D. L., Bullard, K. M., Neighbors, H. W., Geronimus, A. T., Yang, J., & Jackson, J. S. (2012). Are benefits conferred with greater socioeconomic position undermined by racial discrimination among African American men? *Journal of Men's Health, 9*(2), 127–136.

Hudson, D. L., Neighbors, H. W., Geronimus, A. T., & Jackson, J. S. (2016). Racial discrimination, John Henryism, and depression among African Americans. *Journal of Black Psychology, 42*, 221–243. DOI: 10.1177/0095798414567757

Hurd, N., Sellers, R., Cogburn, C., Butler-Barnes, S., & Zimmerman, M. (2013). Racial identity and depressive symptoms among Black emerging adults: The moderating effects of neighborhood racial composition. *Developmental Psychology, 49*, 938–950.

Iwelunmor, J., Idris, O., Adelakun, A., & Airhihenbuwa, C. O. (2010). Child malaria treatment decisions by mothers of children less than five years of age attending an outpatient clinic in southwest Nigeria: An application of the PEN-3 cultural model. *Malaria Journal, 9*, 354–360. http://www.malariajournal.com/content/9/1/354

Jackson, G. G. (1976). The African genesis of the Black perspective in helping. *Professional Psychology*, 292–308.

James, S. A. (1994). John Henryism and the health of African Americans. *Culture, Medicine, and Psychiatry, 18*, 163–182.

James, S. A., Hartnett, S. A., & Kalsbeek, W. D. (1983). John Henryism and blood pressure differences among Black men. *Journal of Behavioral Medicine, 6*, 259–278.

Jaschik, S. (2021, February 22). *Rhetorical support over concrete programs?* Inside Higher Ed. https://www.insidehighered.com/admissions/article/2021/02/22/medical-schools-all-support-black-students-rhetorically-less-half-have

Jerald, M. C., Cole, E. R., Ward, L. M., & Avery, L. R. (2017). Controlling images: How awareness of group stereotypes affects Black women's well-being. *Journal of Counseling Psychology, 64*(5), 487–499. https://doi.org/10.1037/cou0000233

Johnson, E. J., & Rodrigues, V. (2016). Primary health care: Expectations and tasks for public health in Trinidad and Tobago. *Journal of Community Health, 41*, 645–649.

Johnson, R. L. (2002). The relationships among racial identity, self-esteem, sociodemographics, and health promoting lifestyles. *Research and Theory for Nursing Practice: An International Journal, 16*(3), 193–207.

Jonas, K., Duby, Z., Maruping, K., Dietrich, J., Slingers, N., Harries, J., Kuo, C., & Mathews, C. (2020). Perceptions of contraception services among recipients of a combination HIV prevention interventions for adolescent girls and young women in South Africa: A qualitative study. *Reproductive Health, 17*, 122–136. https://doi.org/10.1186/s12978-020-00970-3

Jones, M., Hill-Jarrett, T., Latimer, K., Reynolds, A., Garrett, N., Harris, I., Joseph, S., & Jones, A. (2021). The role of coping in the relationship between endorsement of the SBW schema and depressive symptoms among Black women. *Journal of Black Psychology, 47*(7), 578–592.

Jones, M. M., & Saines, M. (2019). The Eighteen of 1918–1919: Black nurses and the great flu pandemic in the United States. *American Journal of Public Health, 109*, 877–884.

Jones, S., Anderson, R., Gaskin-Wasson, A., Sawyer, B., Applewhite, K., & Metzger, I. (2020). From "crib to coffin": Navigating coping from racism-related stress throughout the lifespan of Black Americans. *American Journal of Orthopsychiatry, 90*(2), 267–282. http://dx.doi.org/10.1037/ort0000430

Kambon, K. K. (1992). *The African personality in America: An African-centered framework*. Nubian Nation Publications.

Kambon, K. K. (1998). *African/Black psychology in the American context: An African-centered approach.* Nubian Nation Publications.

Kelly, B. J., Southwall, B. G., McCormack, L. A., Bann, C. M., MacDonald, P. D., Frasier, A. M., Bevc, C. A., Brewer, N. T., & Squiers, L. B. (2021). Predictors of willingness to get a COVID-19 vaccine in the U.S. *BMC Infectious Diseases, 21,* 338–345.

Kidanemariam, A. (2011). Rethinking health promotion and disease prevention in Africa: The quest for an integrated model. *Journal of Third World Studies, 28*(2), 161–178.

Kiviniemi, M. T., Klasko-Foster, L. B., Erwin, D. O., & Jandorf, L. (2018). Decision-making and socioeconomic disparities in colonoscopy screening in African Americans. *Health Psychology, 37*(5), 481–490. https://doi.org/10.1037/hea0000603

Klasko-Foster, L. B., Jandorf, L. M., Erwin, D. O., & Kiviniemi, M. T. (2019). Predicting colonoscopy screening behavior and future screening intentions for African Americans older than 50 years. *Behavioral Medicine, 45*(3), 221–230. https://doi.org/10.1080/08964289.2018.1510365

KobigBilla, Y. H. (2021, May 2). *Dr. Sulley Gariba goes home.* My Joy Online. https://www.myjoyonline.com/dr-sulley-gariba-goes-home

Krishnan, L., Ogunwole, S. M., & Cooper, L. A. (2020). Historical insights on coronavirus disease 2019 (COVID-19), the 1918 influenza pandemic, and racial disparities: Illuminating a path forward. *Annals of Internal Medicine, 173*(6), 474–481. https://doi.org/10.7326/M20-2223

LaMorte, W. W. (2016, June 8). *Institutional review boards and the Belmont principles.* Boston University. https://sphweb.bumc.bu.edu/otlt/MPH-Modules/EP/EP713_ResearchEthics/EP713_ResearchEthics3.html

Landor, A. M., Simons, L. G., Granberg, E. M., & Melby, J. N. (2019). Colorizing self-esteem among African American young women: Linking skin tone, parental support and sexual health. *Journal of Child and Family Studies, 28,* 1886–1898.

Landrine, H., & Klonoff, E. A. (1996). The schedule of racist events: A measure of racial discrimination and a study of its negative physical and mental health consequences. *Journal of Black Psychology, 22*(2), 144–168.

Lauby, J., Milnamow, M., Joseph, H. A., Hitchcock, S., Carson, L., Pan, Y., Mendoza, M., & Millett, G. (2018). Evaluation of Project RISE, an HIV prevention intervention for Black bisexual men using an ecosystems approach. *AIDS Behavior, 22,* 164–177. https://doi.org/10.1007/s10461-017-1892-5

Lee, D. B., Anderson, R. E., Hope, M. O., & Zimmerman, M. A. (2020). Racial discrimination trajectories predicting psychological well-being: From emerging adulthood to adulthood. *Developmental Psychology, 56*(7), 1413–1423.

Lee, D. B., Kim, E. S., & Neblett, E. W., Jr. (2017). The link between discrimination and telomere length in African American adults. *Health Psychology, 36*(5), 458–467. http://dx.doi.org/10.1037/hea0000450

Lei, M., Beach, S., & Simons, R. (2018). Childhood trauma, pubertal timing, and cardiovascular risk in adulthood. *Health Psychology, 37*(7), 613–617.

Lewis, J. A., Williams, M. G., Peppers, E. J., & Gadson, C. A. (2017). Applying inter-sectionality to explore the relations between gendered racism and health among Black women. *Journal of Counseling Psychology, 64*(5), 475–486.

Lewis, M., Akhu, A., & Hunter, C. (2021). Advancing African psychology: An exploration of African American college students' definitions and use of spirit in times of stress. *Journal of Black Psychology, 47*(7), 507–541.

Li, M. J., Frank, H. G., Harawa, N. T., Williams, J. K., Chou, C., & Blumenthal, R. N. (2018). Racial pride and condom use in post-incarcerated African American men who have sex with men and women: Test of a conceptual model for the Men in Life Environments intervention. *Archives of Sexual Behavior, 47*, 169–181. https://doi.org/10.1007/s10508-016-0734-2

Lightfoot, M., & Milburn, N. (2009). HIV prevention and African American youth: Examination of individual-level behavior is not the only answer. *Culture, Health, and Sexuality, 11*, 731–742.

Linnan, L., & Ferguson, Y. (2007). Beauty salons: A promising health promotion setting for reaching and promoting health among African American women. *Health Education and Behavior, 34*, 517–530.

Locke, T. F., & Newcomb, M. D. (2008). Correlates and predictors of HIV risk among inner-city African American female teenagers. *Health Psychology, 27*(3), 337–348.

Lucas, T., Manning, M., Hayman, L. W., Jr., & Blessman, J. (2018). Targeting and tailoring message framing: The moderating effect of racial identity on receptivity to colorectal cancer screening among African Americans. *Journal of Behavioral Medicine, 41*, 747–756. https://doi.org/10.1007/s10865-018-9933-8

Lumpkins, C. Y., Greiner, K. A., Daley, C., Mabachi, N., & Neuhaus, K. (2013). Promoting healthy behavior from the pulpit: Clergy share their perspectives on effective health communication in the African American church. *Journal of Religious Health, 52*, 1093–1107.

Ly, D. P. (2018). Historical trends in the representativeness and incomes of Black physicians. *Journal of General Internal Medicine.* DOI: 10.1007/s11606-021-06745-1

Madhere, S., Harrell, J., & Royal, C. (2009). Social ecology, genomics, and African American health: A nonlinear dynamical perspective. *Journal of Black Psychology, 35*, 154–179.

Mandara, J., Gaylord-Harden, N. K., Richards, M. H., & Ragsdale, B. L. (2009). The effects of changes in racial identity and self-esteem on changes in African American adolescents' mental health. *Child Development, 80*(6), 1660–1675.

Manove, E. E., Lowe, S. R., Bonumwezi, J., Preston, J., Waters, M. C., & Rhodes, J. E. (2019). Posttraumatic growth in low-income Black mothers who survived Hurricane Katrina. *American Journal of Orthopsychiatry, 89*(2), 144–158. https://doi.org/10.1037/ort0000398

Markovic, N., Bunker, C. H., Ukoli, F. A.M., & Kuller, L. H. (1998). John Henryism and blood pressure among Nigerian civil servants. *Journal of Epidemiology and Community Health, 52*, 186–190.

Masi, C., & Gehlert, S. (2008). Perceptions of breast cancer treatment among African American women and men: Implications for interventions. *Journal of General Internal Medicine, 24*, 408–414.

Masuda, A., Anderson, P., & Sheehan, S. (2009). Mindfulness and mental health among African American college students. *Complementary Health Practice Review, 14*, 115–127.

Matiasha, F. S. (2021, March 1). *COVID-19 vaccines face a trust gap against some traditional African remedies.* Quartz. https://qz.com/africa/1978170/in-zimbabwe-covid-19-vaccine-competes-with-herbal-remedies

Mays, V., Coleman, L., & Jackson, J. (1996). Perceived race-based discrimination, employment status, and job stress in a national sample of Black women: Implications for health outcomes. *Journal of Occupational Health Psychology, 1*(3), 319–329.

McBride, D. F. (2013). Uplifting the family: African American parents' ideas of how to integrate religion into family health programming. *Journal of Child and Family Studies, 22*, 161–173. DOI: 10.1007/s10826-012-9654-5

McDuffie, D. L. (2021). Addressing the mental health of Black older adults during the COVID-19 pandemic. *The Journal of Gerontopsychology and Geriatric Psychiatry.* https://doi.org/10.1024/1662–9647/a000275

McMahon, S. D., & Watts, R. J. (2002). Ethnic identity in urban African American youth: Exploring links with self-worth, aggression, and other psychosocial variables. *Journal of Community Psychology, 30*(4), 411–431.

Mitchell-Jackson, A. (1983). The Black patient and traditional psychotherapy: Implications and possible extensions. *Journal of Community Psychology, 11*(4), 303–307.

Moody, D. L. B., Taylor, A. D., Leibel, D. K., Al-Najjar, E., Katzel, L. I., Davatzikos, C., Gullapalli, R. P., Seliger, S. L., Kovo, T., Erus, G., Rosenberger, W. F., Evans, M. K., Zonderman, A. B., & Waldstein, S. R. (2019). Lifetime discrimination, racial discrimination, and subclinical cerebrovascular disease among African Americans. *Health Psychology, 38*(1), 63–74. http://dx.doi.org/10.1037/hea0000738

Moore, A. P., Rivas, C. A., Stanton-Fay, S., Harding, S., & Goff, L. M. (2019). Designing the Healthy Eating and Active Lifestyles for Diabetes (HEAL-D) self-management and support programme for UK African and Caribbean communities: A culturally tailored, complex intervention underpinned by behavior change theory. *BMC Public Health, 19*, 1146–1160.

Morgan, S. (2004). The power of talk: African Americans' communication with family members about organ donation and its impact on the willingness to donate organs. *Journal of Social and Personal Relationships, 21*, 112–124.

Mouzon, D., & McLean, J. (2017). Internalized racism and mental health among African American, U.S. born Caribbean Blacks, and foreign-born Caribbean Blacks. *Ethnicity and Health, 22*, 36–48. DOI: 10.1080/13557858.2016.1196652

Mukherjee, S. (2021, February 22). Why does the pandemic seem to be hitting some countries harder than others? *The New Yorker.* https://www.newyorker.com/magazine/2021/03/01/why-does-the-pandemic-seem-to-be-hitting-some-countries-harder-than-others

Mushonga, D. R., & Henneberger, A. K. (2019). Protective factors associated with positive mental health in traditional and non-traditional Black students. *American Journal of Orthopsychiatry, 90*(1), 147–160. http://dx.doi.org/10.1037/ort0000409

Mushonga, D. R., Rasheem, S., & Anderson, D. (2021). And still I rise: Resilience factors contributing to post-traumatic growth in African American women. *Journal of Black Psychology, 47*(2–3), 151–176.

Myers, L. J. (1993). *Understanding an Afrocentric world view: Introduction to optimal psychology* (2nd ed.). Kendall Hunt.

Nadimpalli, S. B., James, B. D., Yu, L., Cothran, F., & Barnes, L. L. (2015). The association between discrimination and depressive symptoms among older African Americans: The role of psychological and social factors. *Experimental Aging Research, 41*, 1–24. DOI: 10.1080/0361073x.2015.978201

Nasim, A., Belgrave, F. Z., Jagers, R. J., Wilson, K. D., & Owens, K. (2007). The moderating effects of culture on peer deviance and alcohol use among high-risk African American adolescents. *Journal of Drug Education, 37*(3), 335–363.

National Park Service. (n.d.). *The Legend of John Henry: Talcott, WV*. Retrieved February 13, 2023, from https://www.nps.gov/neri/planyourvisit/the-legend-of -john-henry-talcott-wv.htm

Nazroo, J., Jackson, J., Karlsen, S., & Torres, M. (2007). The Black diaspora and health inequalities in the U.S. and England: Does where you go and how you get there make a difference? *Sociology of Health and Illness, 29*(6), 811–830. doi: 10.1111/j.1467–9566.2007.01043.x

Nyembezi, A., Resnicow, K., Ruiter, R. A.C., van den Borne, B., Sifunda, S., Funani, I., & Reddy, P. (2014). The association between ethnic identity and condom use among young men in the Eastern Cape Province, South Africa. *Archives of Sexual Behavior, 43*, 1097–1103. DOI: 10.1007/s10508-014-0307-1

Ojelade, I., McCray, K., Ashby, J., & Meyers, J. (2011). Use of Ifá as a means of addressing mental health concerns among African American clients. *Journal of Counseling and Development, 89*, 406–412.

Okwumabua, J. O., Wong, S. P., Duryea, E. J., Okwumabua, T. M., & Howell, S. (1999). Building self-esteem through social skills training and cultural awareness: A community-based approach for preventing violence among African American youth. *Journal of Primary Prevention, 20*(1), 61–74.

Opara, I., Rodas, E. I.R., Garcia-Reid, P., & Reid, R. J. (2020). Ethnic identity, empowerment, social support, and sexual risk behaviors among Black adolescent girls: Examining drug use as a mediator. *Child and Adolescent Social Work Journal.* https://doi.org/10.1007/s10560-020-00706-z

Parker, J. S., Haskins, N., Lee, A., Hailemeskel, R., & Adepoju, O. A. (2021). Black adolescents perceptions of COVID-19: Challenges coping, and connection to family, religious, and school support. *School Psychology 36*(5), 303–312.

Patterson, C. E. (2021). Health advocacy at historically Black colleges and universities as social activism. *Phylon, 58*(1/2), 21–38.

Pender. N. (2011). *The Health Promotion Model Manual*. Retrieved from https://deep-blue.lib.umich.edu/bitstream/handle/2027.42/85350/HEALTH_PROMOTION_ MANUAL_Rev_5-2011.pdf?sequence=1&isAllowed=y

Pierce, J., Zhdanova, L., & Lucas, T. (2018). Positive and negative affectivity, stress, and well-being in African-Americans: Initial demonstration of a polynomial regression and response surface methodology approach. *Psychology & Health, 33*(4), 445–464. https://doi.org/10.1080/08870446.2017.1368510

Piper, K. N., Fuller, T. J., Ayers, A. A., Lambert, D. N., Sales, J. M., & Wingood, G. M. (2020). A qualitative exploration of religion, gender norms, and sexual decision making within African American faith-based communities. *Sex Roles, 82*, 189–205. https://doi.org/10.1007/s11199-019-01047-7

Priest, J. B., McNeil Smith, S., Woods, S. B., & Roberson, P. N. E. (2020). Discrimination, family emotional climate, and African American health: An application of the BBFM. *Journal of Family Psychology, 34*(5), 598–609. https://doi.org/10.1037/fam0000621

Prosper, T., Gushue, G. V., & Lee, T. R. (2021). Promoting African American activism: Experiences of racism-related stress and spirituality. *Journal of Black Psychology, 47*(8), 657–668.

Pyant, C., & Yanico, B. (1991). Relationship of racial identity and gender role attitudes to Black women's psychological well-being. *Journal of Counseling Psychology, 38*(3), 315–322.

Reifschneider, M. (2018). Enslavement and institutionalized care: The politics of health in nineteenth-century St Croix, Danish West Indies. *World Archaelogy, 50*(3), 494–511. https://doi.org/10.1080/00438243.2018.1459204

Renzaho, A. M. N., Halliday, J. A., Mellor, D., & Green, J. (2015). The Healthy Migrant Families Initiative: Development of a culturally competent obesity prevention intervention for African migrants. *BMC Public Health, 15*, 272–283. DOI: 10.1186/s12889-015-1628-2

Richman, J., & Fraser, M. (Eds.). (2001). *The context of youth violence: Resilience, risk, and protection.* Praeger Publishing.

Robinson, B. E., Scheltema, K., & Cherry, T. (2005). Risky sexual behavior in low-income African American women: The impact of sexual health variables. *Journal of Sex Research, 42*(3), 224–237.

Robinson, M. A., Kim, I., Mowbray, O., & Washington, T. (2020). The effects of hopelessness on chronic disease among African Americans and Caribbean Blacks: Findings from the National Survey of American Life (NSAL). *Community Mental Health Journal, 56*, 753–759. https://doi.org/10.1007/s10597-019-00536-z

Robinson, M. N., & Thomas Tobin, C. S. (2021). Is John Henryism a health risk or resource? Exploring the role of culturally relevant coping for physical and mental health among Black Americans. *Journal of Health and Social Behavior, 62*, 136–151. doi:10.1177/00221465211009142.

Robinson, W. L., Case, M. H., Whipple, C. R., Gooden, A. S., Lopez-Tamayo, R., Lambert, S. F., & Jason, L. A. (2016). Culturally grounded stress reduction and suicide prevention for African American adolescents. *Practice Innovations, 1*(2), 117–128. http://dx.doi.org/10.1037/pri0000020l

Rose, D. (2011). Captive audience? Strategies for acquiring food in two Detroit neighborhoods. *Qualitative Health Research, 21*(5), 642–651.

Rutter, M. (2001). Psychosocial adversity: Risk, resilience, and recovery. In J. Richman & M. Fraser (Eds.), *The context of youth violence: Resilience, risk, and protection* (pp. 13–42). Praeger Publishing.

Sabik, N., & Versey, H. S. (2016). Functional limitations, body perceptions, and health outcomes among older African American women. *Cultural Diversity and Ethnic Minority Psychology, 22*(4), 594–601. http://dx.doi.org/10.1037/cdp0000106

Sayej, N. (2018, April 21). J Marion Sims: controversial statue taken down but debate still rages. *The Guardian.* https://www.theguardian.com/artanddesign/2018/apr/21/j-marion-sims-statue-removed-new-york-city-black-women

Sellers, R. M., Smith, M. A., Shelton, J. N., Rowley, S. A. J., & Chavous, T. M. (1998). Multidimensional model of racial identity: A reconceptualization of African American racial identity. *Personality and Social Psychology Review, 2*(1), 18–39.

Settles, I. H., Navarrete, C. D., Pagano, S. J., Abdou, C. M., & Sidanius, J. (2010). Racial identity and depression among African American women. *Cultural Diversity and Ethnic Minority Psychology*, 16(2), 248–255. DOI: 101037/a0016442

Sgaier, S., & Downey, J. (2021, November 11). What we see in the shameful trends on U.S. maternal health. *New York Times.* https://www.nytimes.com/interactive/2021/11/17/opinion/maternal-pregnancy-health.html

Shell-Duncan, B., Moreau, A., Wander, K., & Smith, S. (2018). The role of older women in contesting norms associated with female genital mutilation/cutting in Senegambia: A factorial focus group analysis. *PLoS ONE, 13*(7), 1–19.

Sidibe, T., Turner, K., Sparks, A., Woods-Jaeger, B., & Lightfoot, A. (2018). "You still got to see where she's coming from": Using photovoice to understand African American female adolescents' perspectives on sexual risk. *Journal of Early Adolescence, 38*(1), 12–27.

Singh, S. (2004). Resistance, essentialism, and empowerment in Black nationalist discourse in the African diaspora: A comparison of the Back to Africa, Black Power, and Rastafari Movements. *Journal of African American Studies, 8*, 18–36.

Smith, A., & Lalonde, R. (2003). "Racelessness" in a Canadian context? Exploring the link between Black students' identity, achievement, and mental health. *Journal of Black Psychology, 29*(2), 142–164. DOI: 10.1177/0095798403251287

Sobers, N. A., Unwin, N., Samuels, T. A., Capewell, S., O'Flaherty, M., & Critchley, J. A. (2019). Adverse risk factor trends limit gains in coronary heart disease mortality in Barbados: 1990–2012. *PLoS ONE, 14*(4). https://doi.org/10.1371/journal.pone.0215392

Song, L., Hamilton, J. B., & Moore, A. D. (2012). Patient-healthcare provider communication: Perspectives of African American cancer patients. *Health Psychology, 31*(5), 539–547.

Spencer, M. B., Dupree, D., & Hartmann, T. (1997). A phenomenological variant of ecological systems theory: A self-organization perspective in context. *Development and Psychopathology, 9*, 817–833.

Stansbury, K. L., Marshall, G. L., Hall, J., Simpson, G. M., & Bullock, K. (2018). Community engagement with African American clergy: Faith-based model for culturally competent practice. *Aging and Mental Health, 22*(11), 1510–1515.

Stephens, C. (2009). Racism and inequalities in health: Notes toward an agenda for critical health psychology. *Journal of Health Psychology, 14*, 655–659.

Stevenson, H. C., Jr. (1994). Racial socialization in African American families: The art of balancing intolerance and survival. *The Family Journal: Counseling and Therapy for Couples and Families, 2*(3), 190–198.

Stevenson, H. C., Herrero-Taylor, T., Cameron, R., & Davis, G. Y. (2002). "Mitigating instigation": Cultural phenomenological influences of anger and fighting among "big-boned" and "baby-faced" African American youth. *Journal of Youth and Adolescence, 31*, 473–485.

Stock, M. L., Gibbons, F. X., Walsh, L. A., & Gerrard, M. (2011). Racial identification, racial discrimination, and substance use vulnerability among African American young adults. *Personality and Social Psychology Bulletin, 37*(10), 1349–1361.

Street, J., Harris-Britt, A., & Walker-Barnes, C. (2009). Examining relationships between ethnic identity, family environment and psychological outcomes for African American adolescents. *Journal of Child and Family Studies, 18*, 412–420.

Swanson, D. P., Spencer, M. B., Dell'Angelo, T., Harpalani, V., & Spencer, T. (2002). Identity processes and the positive youth development of African Americans: An explanatory framework. *New Directions for Youth Development, 95*, 73–99.

Taggart, T., Powell, W., Gottfredson, N., Ennett, S., Eng, E., & Chatters, L. (2019). A person-centered approach to the study of Black adolescent religiosity, racial identity, and sexual initiation. *Journal of Research on Adolescence, 29*(2), 402–413.

TED. (2016, March 4). *Dorothy Roberts: The problem with race-based medicine.* [Video]. YouTube. https://www.youtube.com/watch?v=KxLMjn4WPBY

Thomas, A., & Sillen, S. (1972). *Racism and psychiatry.* Brunner Mazel.

Thompson, S., & Chambers, J. W. (2000). African self-consciousness and health-promoting behaviors among African American college students. *Journal of Black Psychology, 26*(3), 330–345. https://doi.org/10.1177/0095798400026003005

Tobin, K., Edwards, C., Flath, N., Lee, A., Tormohlen, K., & Gaydos, C. A. (2018). Acceptability and feasibility of a Peer Mentor program to train young Black men who have sex with men to promote HIV and STI home-testing to their social network members. *AIDS Care, 30*(7), 896–902. DOI: 10.1080/09540121.2018.1442553

Toldson, I. L., & Toldson, I. A. (2001). Biomedical ethics: An African-centered psychological perspective. *Journal of Black Psychology, 27*(4), 401–423.

Tolmach, J. (1985). "There ain't nobody on my side": A new day treatment program for Black urban youth. *Journal of Clinical Child Psychology, 14*(3), 214–219. https://doi.org/10.1207/s15374424jccp1403_8

Turner, C., & Darity, W. A. (1973). Fears of genocide among Black Americans as related to age, sex, and region. *American Journal of Public Health, 63*(12), 1029–1034.

Turner-Musa, J., & Wilson, S. (2006). Religious orientation and social support on health promoting behaviors of African American college students. *Journal of Community Psychology, 34*, 105–115.

Vazsonyi, A. T., Pickering, L. E., & Bolland, J. M. (2006). Growing up in a dangerous developmental milieu: The effects of parenting processes on adjustment in inner-city African American adolescents. *Journal of Community Psychology, 34*, 47–73.

Wallace, S. A., & Fisher, C. B. (2007). Substance use attitudes among urban Black adolescents: The role of parent, peer, and cultural factors. *Journal of Youth and Adolescence, 36*, 441–451.

Wamsley, L. (2021, February 18). American life expectancy dropped by a full year in 1st half of 2020. *NPR.* https://www.npr.org/2021/02/18/968791431/american-life-expectancy-dropped-by-a-full-year-in-the-first-half-of-2020

Warren, R. C., Williams, L. S., & Wilson, W. D. (2012). Addressing the legacy of the U.S. Public Health Service syphilis study at Tuskegee: Optimal health in health care reform philosophy. *Ethics and Behavior, 22*(6), 496–500.

Warren-Findlow, J., Laditka, J., Laditka, L., & Thompson, M. E. (2011). Association between social relationships and emotional well-being in middle-aged and older African Americans. *Research on Aging, 33*(6), 713–734.

Weaver, K. K. (2012). Surgery, slavery, and the circulation of knowledge in the French Caribbean. *Slavery and Abolition, 33*(1), 105–117.

Whaley, A. L. (2003). Cognitive-cultural model of identity and violence prevention for African American youth. *Genetic, Social, and General Psychology Monographs, 129*(2), 101–151.

Whaley, A. L., & McQueen, J. P. (2020). Evaluating Africentric violence prevention for adolescent Black males in an urban public school: An idiothetic approach. *Journal of Child and Family Studies, 29*, 942–954. https://doi.org/10.1007/s10826-019-01637-9

Whoriskey, P. (2020, October 22). The bogus U.S. census numbers showing slavery's "wonderful influence" on the enslaved. IBW21. https://ibw21.org/reparations/bogus-us-census-showing-slaverys-wonderful-influence-on-the-enslaved

Wood, B. L. (1994). One articulation of the structural family therapy model: A biobehavioral family model of chronic illness in children. *Journal of Family Therapy, 16*(1), 53–72. https://doi.org/10.1111/j.1467-6427.1994.00777.x

Woolford, S. J., Woolford-Hunt, C. J., Sami, A., Blake, N., & Williams, D. R. (2016). No sweat: African American adolescent girls' opinions of hairstyle choices and physical activity. *BMC Obesity, 3*(31), 1–8. DOI: 10.1186/s40608-016-0111-7

Wooster, J., Eshel, A., Moore, A., Mishra, M., Toledo, C., Uhi, G., & Wright-DeAguero, L. (2011). Opening up their doors: Perspectives on the involvement of the African American faith community in HIV prevention in four communities. *Health Promotion Practice, 12*(5), 769–778. DOI: 10.1177/1524839910362313?utm

Worrell, F. C., Vandiver, B. J., Cross, W. E., Jr., & Fhagen-Smith, P. E. (2004). Reliability and structural validity of cross racial identity scale scores in a sample of African American adults. *Journal of Black Psychology, 30*(4), 489–505. https://doi.org/10.1177/0095798404268281

Zapolski, T. C. B., Beutlich, M. R., Fisher, S., & Barnes-Najor, J. (2018). Collective ethnic-racial identity and health outcomes among African American youth: Examination of promotive and protective effects. *Cultural Diversity and Ethnic Minority Psychology, 25*(3), 388–396.

# Index

# About the Author

**Marilyn D. Lovett** has over 25 years of experience in higher education as a faculty member and an administrator. She is currently coordinator of Africana studies and associate professor of psychological science at Valdosta State University. Her doctoral degree in social psychology was earned at the University of Cincinnati, and her undergraduate (psychology) and master's (community psychology) degrees are from Florida A&M University. She enjoys sharing her research in health promotion and cultural identity, which she has presented at community forums and professional conferences, while her publications range from encyclopedia entries to articles in peer-reviewed journals.

Printed in the USA
CPSIA information can be obtained
at www.ICGtesting.com
LVHW041234291023
762360LV00004B/89